Fruit
of the Spirit

Published by Barbour Publishing, Inc., P.O. Box 719, Uhrichsville, Ohio 44683, www.barbourbooks.com

Our mission is to publish and distribute inspirational products offering exceptional value and biblical encouragement to the masses.

Member of the
Evangelical Christian
Publishers Association

Printed in China.

Inspiration for Women from
Galatians 5:22–23

Fruit
of the
Spirit

MARCIA HORNOK

BARBOUR
PUBLISHING

Contents

Walk by the Spirit, and you will not gratify the desires of the flesh. For the desires of the flesh are against the Spirit, and the desires of the Spirit are against the flesh, for these are opposed to each other, to keep you from doing the things you want to do. But if you are led by the Spirit, you are not under the law. . . . The fruit of the Spirit is love, joy, peace, patience, kindness, goodness, faithfulness, gentleness [meekness], self-control; against such things there is no law. And those who belong to Christ Jesus have crucified the flesh with its passions and desires. If we live by the Spirit, let us also keep in step with the Spirit. Let us not become conceited, provoking one another, envying one another.

GALATIANS 5:16–18, 22–26 ESV

Introduction

Fruit-bearing Christian women live in fellowship with Christ like a branch connected to a grapevine. This daily dependence on God enables us to live out righteousness instead of give in to the desires of our flesh as Galatians 5 details. When we do this, God, the Holy Spirit, develops His fruit in our lives.

This book will encourage and equip you to depend on God and experience His love, joy, and peace in your relationship with Him; His patience, gentleness, and goodness in your relations with others; and His faithfulness, meekness, and self-control with regard to yourself.

Fruit Happens

*But the fruit of the Spirit is love, joy, peace,
patience, kindness, goodness, faithfulness,
gentleness [meekness], self-control. . . .
And those who belong to Christ Jesus have
crucified the flesh with its passions and desires.*
GALATIANS 5:22–24 ESV

How do I get the fruit of the Spirit in my life?
The same way the works of the flesh (sinful
nature) happen—by my conduct, resulting
from my choices. Thus God exhorts us to yield
ourselves to the Spirit, not the flesh (Romans
6; 12:1–2). When our choices are loving, joyful,
peaceful, patient, God grows His fruit in us.

John 15 portrays a grapevine. We are a branch
connected to Christ the vine. Abiding in Christ
means fellowshipping with Him throughout
our day's activities. Like a toddler who wants to
stay near her mother, we should mentally run to
God every time our mind is not engaged with

something else. This produces in us the character of Christ (spiritual fruit), and also prevents our flesh from dictating our conduct.

What is the purpose of fruit? It showcases the vinedresser, not ourselves, and it nourishes everyone with whom we interact. How do we know we have the Spirit's fruit? If we submit our life to God every morning and stay in fellowship with Him as we face our daily ups and downs, then fruit happens. Our actions, words, and attitudes will show it. That is what yielding to the Spirit means—also called walking (v. 16), being led (v. 18), living by the Spirit, and keeping in step with the Spirit (v. 25).

Abiding in Christ keeps our choices and actions loving, joyful, peaceful, patient, kind, good, faithful, meek, and self-controlled.

Love Is Kind

Love is not touchy.

ELISABETH ELLIOT, *LET ME BE A WOMAN*

Making Love Happen

And now these three remain: faith, hope and love.
But the greatest of these is love.
1 CORINTHIANS 13:13 NIV

Is love something that happens to us or something we make happen? Most people marry because they love each other and want to spend their lives together. But most couples who divorce claim they don't love each other anymore. Love seems to come and go depending on our feelings and our response to circumstances.

God's love, however, is constant. It is patient and kind. It rejoices over truth. It always protects and trusts, hopes and endures. God's love in us also helps us resist doing harmful things like envying, boasting about ourselves, putting ourselves first, dishonoring others, seeking attention, getting angry easily, holding grudges, and delighting in evil. Many couples hear "The Love Chapter" (1 Corinthians 13) read during their wedding ceremony. It reminds them that love never fails when they practice the positive behaviors and resist the negative ones given in this chapter.

Yet at times we do feel like we have fallen out of love with our spouse or family member. What should we do then? Revelation 2:5 gives the prescription for rekindling the love we used to have: remember, repent, and redo the works we did when we felt love for that person. Feelings follow actions. If we've "lost that loving feeling," we can find it again when we apply God's love to our relationships. Start by practicing the characteristics of 1 Corinthians 13, a few at a time. Love happens when we make it happen.

Daddy's Girl

"The LORD your God in your midst, the Mighty One, will save; He will rejoice over you with gladness, He will quiet you with His love, He will rejoice over you with singing."

ZEPHANIAH 3:17 NKJV

Imagine how God loves us according to this verse. The context is restoration after chastisement. God calls Israel His daughter who has turned from disobedience (Zephaniah 3:2) and corruption (v. 7) and has learned to humbly trust Him (v. 12). He tells Israel, "Be glad and rejoice with all your heart, O daughter of Jerusalem!" (v. 14 NKJV).

Scene one: You are God's little girl, running to meet Him. He kneels on one knee and extends His arms to grab you in a bear hug. See His big smile as He says, "I'm so glad to see you, my sweet girl."

Scene two: You suddenly scream. A bee has stung your hand. Shocked and puzzled, you're inconsolable. But God picks you up, kisses the bee-stung place, and speaks low in your ear: "It's okay, sweetie, I'm here. Don't cry. Daddy loves you."

Scene three: He holds you on His lap and sings your special song—the one He made up just for you. It has your name in it, and you love hearing Him sing it.

That's what Zephaniah 3:17 looks like for today's woman. That's how God's relationship feels in our lives. He loves us totally. He quiets us gently when we hurt. He enjoys being with us and delights in us.

No matter what kind of home you grew up in, or how flawed your dad was, you have a caring Father who loves you unconditionally. Rejoice in God's love, because God rejoices over you.

Loving the Unseen

Though you have not seen him, you love him.
1 PETER 1:8 NIV

In a long-distance relationship with a friend or relative, we love what we cannot see. Mutual love grows as two people communicate, do special things for each other, and think positively about their shared history.

In a sense, our relationship with God is long distance. How do we nurture it? Mainly by prayer (talking to Him) and Bible reading (Him talking to us). Many Christians do this regularly in a devotional time. They may also include Christian music, journaling, or a Bible study book. However, we need more than a time for *devotions* that we cross off our daily to-do list. We also need daily *devotion.* Each of us must train our mind to run to God when it is not otherwise occupied. Do you have a measuring tape with a button that makes the tape snap back to its source? Our minds can be like that tape measure, snapping back to God at every pause in our thinking.

Devotion to God includes all the things that make our love for Him grow: singing and making melody in our hearts to Him, listening to Christian teachings and music, memorizing scripture verses, serving Him, and thinking about Him. First Thessalonians 5:17 calls this praying "without ceasing" (ESV).

The more we practice these spiritual disciplines, the more we will love our unseen God. In eternity we will enjoy His physical presence, making our romance with Him complete.

This I Know and Experience

That Christ may dwell in your hearts through faith;
that you, being rooted and grounded in love, may be able
to comprehend with all the saints what is the width and
length and depth and height—to know the love
of Christ which passes knowledge; that you
may be filled with all the fullness of God.
EPHESIANS 3:17–19 NKJV

What is the most profound theological truth you learned in your years of study?" someone asked Karl Barth, a leading theologian of the twentieth century. Barth answered, "Jesus loves me. This I know, for the Bible tells me so." This children's song, written by Anna B. Warner in 1860, contains the most important truth for Christians of all ages.

Ephesians 3 says we want to comprehend His love, yet it surpasses knowledge. Although we can study all the ways Jesus loves us and know something about His love's vast dimensions, that is not enough. We need Jesus' love in our hearts, not only our heads. His love is more than facts—it is relational. The scriptures inform us about His love, but also inspire us to experience it, and be filled with love as a fruit of the Spirit.

Another paradox about our relationship with Christ is that we are in Christ, and yet Christ is in us. To visualize this, take three different-sized envelopes. Write "Jesus" on the smallest one and the largest one. Write your name on the middle-sized one. Put the small one inside the medium one and those inside the big one. There you have it! You in Christ and Christ in you. Incomprehensible, isn't it? Don't try to figure it out—enjoy it.

Does God have your heart today? We love and trust Him, even though we cannot comprehend Him.

Loving God and Neighbors

"Hear, O Israel: The LORD our God, the LORD is one! You shall love the LORD your God with all your heart, with all your soul, and with all your strength."

DEUTERONOMY 6:4–5 NKJV

The Bible's definitive words about love from Deuteronomy 6:4–9 comprise the Shema, pronounced Sh'MAH. This prayer is recited every morning and evening by religious Jews. Steve Herzig says the meaning of the Hebrew word for heart carries "the idea of will or intention." The word for soul includes "the idea of life" and "I must love God with all my strength." The woman who makes this statement of faith and means it would "want to give [her] whole self to God, to hold nothing back. God would own [her]—body, soul, and spirit."[1] Do you have this kind of all-or-nothing love for Him? When you do, it will extend to loving your neighbors as well. In fact, Romans 13:8–10 and Galatians 5:13–14 tell us that loving others fulfills God's whole law.

In Luke 10 an interpreter of Jewish law understood this, but he challenged Jesus by asking, "Who is my neighbor?" Jesus rarely gave a direct answer to a question—He let people draw their own conclusions—so He told this lawyer the Good Samaritan story to show that a merciful neighbor extends help to those in need (Luke 10).

Because God showed mercy to helpless, dying, destitute me, I love Him with all my heart (will), soul (life), and strength (actions). This enables me to be merciful and loving to others who have needs I can meet.

Bonded by Love

And over all these virtues put on love,
which binds them all together in perfect unity.
COLOSSIANS 3:14 NIV

My mother, Mary Ann Noel, wore a girdle under her housedress every day. I guess she needed it after carrying eight babies, including full-term twins. It held everything in, and she didn't feel dressed without it. In Bible times, people wore a band or sash to hold their clothes in place. They could tuck their robes into it when they needed to run or work hard. So when Colossians speaks of love binding the other virtues together, it means we should surround everything we do with love. We won't be fully dressed without it.

The virtues in Colossians 3:12–15 include six aspects of the fruit of the Spirit. We are to "put them on" like a garment and hold them in place with love. First John 5:1–3 says our love for God causes us to love God's children as well, and

Titus 2:4 implies that we can even learn how to love our husband and children better. But loving others is more than a warm feeling; it is things we do (1 John 3:16–18). Dr. Gary Chapman has wisely categorized showing love as five "Love Languages": Words of Affirmation, Quality Time, Physical Touch, Gifts, and Acts of Service.[2] He explains that the way we like to receive love will be the way we tend to express it. However, if others "hear" love differently from the way we offer it, we have a disconnect. Ask God to help you learn to "speak" another's love language. This will bond you together in unity. No girdles necessary!

Loving One Another

This is love: not that we loved God, but that he loved us and sent his Son as an atoning sacrifice for our sins. Dear friends, since God so loved us, we also ought to love one another.
1 JOHN 4:10–11 NIV

Our inspiration for loving others is being loved by God. How does God love us? By forgiving our sins and accepting us as His adopted children. When parents desperately crave a child by adoption, they sacrifice to meet the expenses and diligently wait throughout the long, difficult process. Since God loves us like that, and worked out all the details to bring us into His family, He wants us to share His love with others. How? By forgiving them when they offend us. By sacrificing our time, efforts, and resources to meet their needs. By nurturing our relationship with them over time.

Our love will never be perfect and unconditional like God's, because God is love (1 John 4:8, 16). By His nature He loves, not because anything in us causes Him to. We see this in Deuteronomy 7:6–9, where God did not choose the Israelites because of them, but because He loves, and He keeps His promises. He does, however, desire that people respond by loving Him back and by obeying His commands. One frequently stated command is for us to love one another. He makes this possible by growing His love in us as a fruit of the Spirit.

So even if love was absent from your childhood, or if you don't see yourself as a loving person, and even when a bad day makes you cranky, ask God to show you His love and teach you how to share it with others.

Love Grows

*May the Lord make your love increase and overflow for
each other and for everyone else, just as ours does for you.*
1 Thessalonians 3:12 NIV

"Some people are hard to love," Vonda said after
visiting her dad in his retirement home. "Why
should I keep seeing him when all he does is
criticize and contradict everything I say?" Before
giving up on her dad, Vonda asked God to teach
her how to love him the way he needed to be
loved. The Bible says love increases and grows
because the Lord causes it to. He nurtures His
love in us, and we love Him in return (1 John
4:19). As our source of love, He also makes
it overflow to everyone within our circle of
influence.

That is why 1 Thessalonians 4:9 says, "You
have no need for anyone to write to you, for you
yourselves *are taught by God* to love one another"
(NASB). How does God teach us to love? The same
way we learn any useful skill—by practice, and by

trial and error. God gives generous opportunities for us to express love in both words and actions to our family, neighbors, relatives, strangers, and even to people who treat us with animosity. In fact, only God can enable us to love the unlovable. Every opportunity we respond to increases our ability to overflow with God's love.

As Vonda continued visiting her dad and stopped arguing with him, God helped her accept him and meet his needs. Eventually he began to show appreciation for her.

Ask God to use you today to overflow His love to someone who needs it.

Learning to Walk

Walk in love, as Christ also has loved us and given Himself for us, an offering and a sacrifice to God.
EPHESIANS 5:2 NKJV

How do we learn to walk in love? Remember how a toddler goes from crawling to walking on her own? First she pulls up to furniture. Then as someone holds her hands, she moves her feet. Eventually she stands alone, takes a few wide-legged steps, and falls. Picking herself up, she does it again. Through persistence and practice, she soon becomes steady and sure of her steps.

Learning to walk in love requires the same stumbling process. We reach out to someone, but our efforts backfire. Instead of committing the situation to the Lord, we hold a grudge. Then another need comes along, and we meet it. We give of ourselves seeking nothing in return, but perhaps we struggle with thinking, *This is not worth it. It costs too much and wastes my time. No one appreciates it anyhow, so why should I bother?*

Sometimes we stroll; sometimes we stumble—
it takes effort to love and serve others. However,
by God's provision of love in us, we can sacrifice
and meet needs, because loving others serves Him.
Jesus taught that what we do for "the least of
these," we do for Him (Matthew 25:37–40 NKJV).
Through persistence and practice, we will learn
to welcome opportunities, even when they are
draining. Being "rooted and grounded" in His love
(Ephesians 3:17 NKJV) enables us to put up with
incompetence and messiness in others, because
we see them with God's perspective. Like us, they,
too, are learning to walk.

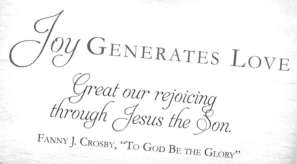

Joy Generates Love

*Great our rejoicing
through Jesus the Son.*

Fanny J. Crosby, "To God Be the Glory"

Words Are Inadequate

Though you do not now see him, you believe in him and rejoice with joy that is inexpressible and filled with glory.
1 PETER 1:8 ESV

Joy, by its nature, requires expression. Rejoicing causes us to clap, jump up and down, or pump our fists while yelling, cheering, whistling, or even crying. How then can joy be inexpressible? In 1 Peter 1:6 we are told to rejoice greatly in our salvation, even though "now for a little while you may have had to suffer grief in all kinds of trials" (NIV). We experience glorious inner joy because of our relationship with Christ, whether it's a happy day or a grievous one.

This joy does not spring from circumstances or feelings. It is spiritual joy, the Spirit's fruit. The adjective translated as *inexpressible* in this verse is related to a word in 2 Corinthians 9:15, "Thanks be to God for his inexpressible gift!" (ESV). God's gracious gift to us of eternal salvation cannot be fully explained through words or understood through reason. We only know two things: we are unworthy, and our life with God will never, never end. This boggles the mind. We will live on and on in eternity. Forever with the Lord!

Not only is God's gift of salvation indescribable, but the settled joy we have as a result is also indescribable. Write a thank-you note to God. Start it by saying, "Words cannot express how much I appreciate Your gift to me. It gives me great joy to think of how You. . ."

Written Joys

Rejoice in the Lord always;
again I will say, rejoice!
PHILIPPIANS 4:4 NASB

God knows that rejoicing changes our perspective, so He commands us to rejoice. His joy grows in us when we fellowship with Him and keep our thoughts on what is true, honorable, right, pure, lovely, and praiseworthy (Philippians 4:8). Focusing on the positive generates joy. When we count our blessings, we begin to feel blessed. Consider writing them down.

Frieda keeps a notebook of answers to prayer and ways God shows up in her circumstances. She reviews it with her family at Thanksgiving or on Christmas Eve. Kay records at least three good things in a journal every night: the first red tomato from the garden, a friend's phone call, an accident avoided, or a spectacular sunset. Often it is something she has done that day to help someone in need, because making others happy yields joy for us, too. She says, "Recording good things keeps my focus off what went wrong and gives me a rejoicing spirit." When Pauline feels discouraged, she sets the timer for one hour and makes a list of things she is thankful for. At first she doubts she can fill an hour, but inevitably, when the timer dings, she doesn't want to stop!

Of course we can always rejoice in who God is and in our relationship with Him—what a privilege! But we can have even more joy and a positive outlook if we daily or periodically keep a record of our blessings. Today, what would you write down?

Joy after Sorrow

"You will grieve, but your grief will turn to joy. . . .
So with you: Now is your time of grief, but I will see you again
and you will rejoice, and no one will take away your joy."
JOHN 16:20, 22 NIV

Jesus reassured His disciples that sorrow was temporary. Little did they know they would soon grieve His death, but after His resurrection, they would have lasting joy.

The world cannot rob us of the joy we have because of Jesus' death and resurrection. When we trust Him for salvation, the consequences of our sins are gone. Our salvation has three aspects of deliverance from sin: We have past deliverance from the *penalty* of sin. A personal relationship with God enables us to have present deliverance from the *power* of sin in our lives. And in eternity, we look forward to future deliverance from the *presence* of sin itself.

The Bible has big spiritual words for it. The

past aspect is called *justification*—God declares us righteous. The present aspect is *sanctification*—the Spirit helps us live a holy life. And the future aspect is *glorification*—we will share Christ's glory. Second Thessalonians 2:13–14 contains all three: "God has chosen you from the beginning for salvation through sanctification by the Spirit and faith in the truth. It was for this He called you through our gospel, that you may gain the glory of our Lord Jesus Christ" (NASB).

In this life we have many sorrows. They steal our happiness, at least for a time, but nothing can rob us of the joy—the sense of well-being—we have in our forever relationship with God.

Fixated on Joy

Fixing our eyes on Jesus, the pioneer and perfecter of faith.
For the joy set before him he endured the cross, scorning
its shame, and sat down at the right hand of the throne
of God. Consider him who endured such opposition from
sinners, so that you will not grow weary and lose heart.
HEBREWS 12:2–3 NIV

What are you looking forward to today? God
formed us in such a way that we cannot sustain
ourselves emotionally without something to hope
in—something to anticipate. Even Jesus looked
ahead as He endured opposition and crucifixion.
He focused on the end result—joy with God the
Father after accomplishing His work on earth.
Perhaps He also found joy from obeying, or
anticipated the joy He will share with us because
His sacrifice paid for our redemption. He may
have thought of the relief of dying, the wonder
of resurrecting, the joy of surprising His friends
and His reunion with them—a reunion that will
someday include us!

We who believe in Christ always have something to look forward to. Even if our current prognosis is death, to die is gain because we will be immediately with the Lord (2 Corinthians 5:8). Not that we want to hurry the process! A joy-centered focus can keep us from despairing over present circumstances and sorrows. It takes determination and spiritual power to meditate on the joys set before us when we'd rather commiserate about our suffering. But the Holy Spirit will help us.

Jesus' suffering on the cross ended in death; our present suffering may not. But everyone who knows Jesus as her Savior can look forward to a joyful eternity where God will wipe away all our tears and compensate all our losses. Until then, He helps us to keep going and not lose heart.

Faulty Thinking Steals Joy

*[You] are being guarded through faith for a salvation
ready to be revealed in the last time. In this you
rejoice, though now for a little while, if necessary,
you have been grieved by various trials.*
1 PETER 1:5–6 ESV

When we're depressed we often want sympathy,
not sermons. We want to withdraw and wallow in
our problems, like Elijah in 1 Kings 19. He was
so depressed that he prayed for death. Elijah had
expected revival in Israel after his great victory
on Mt. Carmel. Instead, King Ahab resolved
to kill him. Elijah told God, "I have been very
zealous for the LORD, the God of hosts; for the
sons of Israel have forsaken Your covenant. . . .
And I alone am left; and they seek my life, to
take it away" (NASB). Unable to see beyond his
circumstances and feelings, he thought he was all
alone and that his work had been wasted.

God sent angels with food to strengthen

him, and also let him sleep. Then God corrected his thinking. God showed him that He is often a God of small beginnings. After all, Elijah had just experienced an "abundance of rain" that had started with a fist-sized cloud (1 Kings 18:41–46 NKJV). But God did not speak through a strong wind, earthquake, or fire, but in a still, small voice. He "whispered" to Elijah that he was not alone— there were still seven thousand Israelites who had not worshipped Baal. Then God gave Elijah a helper, Elisha, to carry on the ministry. Elijah's work would not be in vain. And by the way, Elijah never did die!

When moments of depression steal our joy, we should eat healthy food, get more sleep, and replace our faulty thinking with God's truth. The joy of the Lord will return.

Joy during Persecution

You became imitators of us and of the Lord,
for you welcomed the message in the midst of
severe suffering with the joy given by the Holy Spirit.
1 THESSALONIANS 1:6 NIV

The old Westminster Catechism says, "The chief end of man is to glorify God and enjoy Him forever." In seasons of distress this may seem impossible. God is loving and sovereign, but He does not prevent all suffering. The suspicion that He causes suffering can be horrifying. How do we enjoy God when nothing about our life is joyful?

The Christians in Thessalonica experienced persecution, yet had joy. They were not to let persecution shake them because they were "appointed to" it (1 Thessalonians 3:3 NKJV). Lifestyles and beliefs that clash with popular culture can result in discrimination and even martyrdom. How does that produce joy? Spirit-given joy is possible even while suffering undeservedly. Joy is based on facts about God, so we can have joy in our minds without feeling joy in our emotions. No matter how dark our circumstances seem, we can rejoice in these truths:

God's work. He builds character in us through difficulties.

God's will. He accomplishes His goals in us and through us when we respond with obedience.

God's ways. He harvests joy out of tears (Psalm 126:5–6; 2 Corinthians 6:10), peace out of anxiety (Philippians 4:6–7), strength from weakness (2 Corinthians 12:9–10), and life out of death (2 Corinthians 4:11–12).

God will either deliver us from a trial or sustain us through it. Truly we can "enjoy God forever."

Afterward

All discipline [training] for the moment seems not to be joyful, but sorrowful; yet to those who have been trained by it, afterwards it yields the peaceful fruit of righteousness.
HEBREWS 12:11 NASB

"I have no joy," Marlena told Vicki. "How can I be joyful when my little girl is dying? Joy is a fruit of the Spirit, but I don't see how I'll ever have joy again. I'm too sad."

Vicki could sympathize, because she had lost a child also. "I'm so sorry, Marlena. It hurts severely, and it will hurt for a long time. You will never be the same, but you will get through it. The Bible says we don't have joy during trials, but afterward we will see fruit that results."

Both women paused to wipe their eyes. Then Vicki said, "The fruit of the Spirit isn't determined by our feelings, you know. Joy might be more of an *awareness* that God is with you during this difficult time, and you can lean on Him. Are you still glad that your sins are forgiven and you belong to God?"

"Yes," Marlena said.

"Can you be thankful that God is in control, and no matter what happens, He will take care of you?"

"Yes, but I don't like it!" Marlena admitted.

"Of course not. But I learned that even after a long night of weeping, joy comes in the morning."

Eventually Marlena learned this, too. Through grief, her relationship with God deepened, and feelings of joy returned to partner with her inner awareness of joy.[3]

Our Source of Joy

They offered great sacrifices, and rejoiced,
for God had made them rejoice with great joy;
the women and the children also rejoiced,
so that the joy of Jerusalem was heard afar off.
NEHEMIAH 12:43 NKJV

God had given Israel great joy. Their source of joy, and ours, is God. In Nehemiah 12 the Israelites were dedicating the rebuilt wall around Jerusalem. The event planners brought all the Levites to Jerusalem to celebrate "both with thanksgivings and singing, with cymbals and stringed instruments and harps" (Nehemiah 12:27 NKJV). Two "thanksgiving choirs" sang antiphonally. The people had faced many obstacles and setbacks while building the wall, but Nehemiah told them, "Do not sorrow, for the joy of the LORD is your strength" (Nehemiah 8:10 NKJV).

A study note for Nehemiah 8:10 says: "The joy of the Lord is the joy that springs up in our hearts because of our relationship to the Lord. It is a God-given gladness found when we are in communion with God. When our goal is to know more about the Lord, the by-product is His joy. *Strength* here means 'place of safety,' a 'refuge,' or 'protection.'"[4]

The next time you need a refuge—a safe place—find it by rejoicing in the Lord. A praise chorus says, "It's amazing what praising can do." We can sing ourselves out of a funk. Listen to Christian music. Make a mental or written list of your blessings. Say thank You to God for ten things about your relationship with Him. Meditate on His attributes by thinking of one for each letter from A to Z. His joy will result.

Until Then

*Beloved, do not be surprised at the fiery trial when
it comes upon you to test you, as though something
strange were happening to you. But rejoice insofar
as you share Christ's sufferings, that you may also
rejoice and be glad when his glory is revealed.*
1 PETER 4:12–13 ESV

Fiery trials are our opportunities to share
Christ's sufferings during our earth-life and
participate in Christ's glory in the next life. Joni
Eareckson Tada became quadriplegic at age
seventeen. She said, "The deeper the suffering,
the higher the glory. . .[for those who] honor
Christ with an uncomplaining spirit." Suffering
makes us "more devoted to the future than the
present. More devoted to the spiritual than the
physical. And more devoted to eternal realities
than temporal ones."⁵ When we rejoice in these
things, it keeps us from being resentful or
rebellious. Will we feel thankful? No, but getting
to the point where we can say thank You to God

does not mean we are glad for what happened; it means we accept it. If we obey by thanking God for all things, He is glorified and our attitude is sanctified.

Jesus said in this world we will have tribulation, but we can take heart, because He has overcome the world (John 16:33). Someday we will be with Him forever, and our joy will be full. The "fellowship of His sufferings" mentioned in Philippians 3:10 (NKJV) will be worth it all when He wipes away our tears. Each trial will "result in praise, glory and honor when Jesus Christ is revealed" (1 Peter 1:7 NIV).

Until then, we will endure tribulations and fiery trials. Rejoice in the spiritual benefits they are giving you and the future glory you will share with Christ.

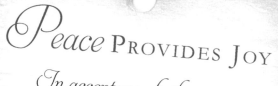

Peace Provides Joy

In acceptance lieth peace:
O my heart be still. Let thy restless
worries cease and accept His will.

Amy Carmichael

Peace Like a River

For to set the mind on the flesh is death,
but to set the mind on the Spirit is life and peace.
ROMANS 8:6 ESV

Horatio Spafford, a successful Christian attorney in Chicago wrote, "When peace like a river attendeth my way, when sorrows like sea billows roll; Whatever my lot, Thou hast taught me to say, 'It is well, it is well with my soul.'" The Spaffords had four daughters and one son. In 1871 their son became ill and died. A short time later the Chicago fire destroyed most of Mr. Spafford's real-estate investments. To encourage his family, he decided they should sail to England, where he could assist D. L. Moody with an evangelistic campaign.

When urgent business detained him, his wife and daughters sailed as scheduled. On November 22, 1873, their ship was struck by another vessel and sank in twelve minutes. Mrs. Spafford cabled her husband: SAVED ALONE. Their daughters

Tanetta, Maggie, Annie, and Bessie had drowned. Horatio immediately sailed to join his wife in Wales. When his ship passed near the area where his daughters had died, he wrote the poem, "It Is Well with My Soul," which later became a beloved hymn.

Horatio and his wife, Anna, had three more children, including another son who died. In 1881 the Spaffords moved to Jerusalem and established a hospitality house for all people—Jews, Christians, and Muslims. It eventually became a children's medical center, still operating today.

During overwhelming grief, let God's peace sustain you and give you the courage to know all is well in your soul.

Shalom

In some church traditions, the speaker says,
"Peace be with you," and the congregation
responds, "And also with you." This mirrors the
Hebrew greeting *shalom*, which extends peace.
Shalom means much more than "hi" or "good-
bye." A good parallel is *aloha*, which captures the
generous Hawaiian way of welcoming, showing
kindness, and giving hospitality.

Newlyweds Jon and Leah moved to Hawaii,
where Jon was stationed with the Air Force. They
rented a basement apartment, and during their
first few months, the landlord brought them
cookies, treats, and fruit multiple times. Whenever
the landlord had a luau party outdoors, and Jon
and Leah happened to walk by, they soon had
plates of food in their hands.

In the same way, shalom does more than acknowledge someone's presence. The root word means "complete, full, or perfect." It wishes a person peace, health, welfare, wholeness, safety, and rest. The blessing of Numbers 6:24–26 correctly attributes shalom-peace to the Lord. He is the only source of complete peace for us. Isaiah 9:6 calls the promised Messiah the "Prince of Peace." When angels announced His coming, they proclaimed, "Glory to God in the highest heaven, and on earth peace to those on whom his favor rests" (Luke 2:14 NIV). Jesus brings us into peace with God in exchange for death and separation caused by our sin.[6]

Having peace with God means we can have peace in our lives and in our relationships—with spouse and relatives, coworkers and neighbors, friends and church peers. Shalom.

Daddy's Home

Just as a father has compassion on his children,
so the LORD has compassion on those who fear Him.
PSALM 103:13 NASB

Mara had a worry habit. Even though she prayed
about everything, she couldn't seem to cast her
cares on God and leave them there. Meditating
on problems, fears for the future, and what-if
questions kept her awake at night.

One day her children were listening to *The
Music Machine* children's musical.[7] The words to
one song spoke to her: "Knowing that my daddy's
home, God gives me peace." The song equates
peace with security, no worries. All is well because
Daddy's here. For the first time, Mara thought
about God being a compassionate Father who
was at home with her, taking care of her monster
worries:

Fear—Daddy protects me.
Anxiety—Daddy provides what I need.

Worry—Daddy can handle anything.
Harm—Daddy keeps me safe.

Although we've all had different experiences with our earthly fathers, God designates Himself as a compassionate father who has everything under control. But we must let Him take control. Then we can rest without worries. Jesus called God *Abba*, father, in Gethsemane. *Abba* may be similar to "papa" or "daddy." Thinking of God this way neutralizes our fears and allows peace to reign. God is in charge of our welfare and safety, our problems and needs.

Knowing this gave Mara a Psalm 4:8 reality: "In peace I will both lie down and sleep, for You alone, O Lord, make me to dwell in safety" (NASB). Will you sleep in peace tonight?[8]

Better Than a Spa

"But the Helper, the Holy Spirit, whom the Father
will send in My name, He will teach you all things. . . .
Peace I leave with you, My peace I give to you;
not as the world gives do I give to you. Let not your
heart be troubled, neither let it be afraid."
JOHN 14:26–27 NKJV

How does the world give peace? An hour-
long massage or spa treatment? A cruise where
stewards anticipate all our needs? A day at the
beach? We tend to associate peacefulness with
being pampered and having no responsibilities
for a time. Jesus does not give peace in the same
way. His peace comes as a fruit of the Holy Spirit,
whom Jesus called the *Paraclete*, which means
"helper or comforter."

Jesus' peace comes from the Spirit, like fruit
from a plant. The Holy Spirit grows it in our heart
when we abide in the vine. God's peace does not
relieve us of responsibilities. Instead, it enables
us to accomplish them without being troubled or

fearful. Jesus told his disciples, "Do not let your heart be troubled; believe in God, believe also in Me" (John 14:1 NASB). When we have a troubled or fearful heart, we should examine what we are believing: Is it God's truth, or is it a lie based on the world, our flesh (sinful nature), or Satan?

Although pampering ourselves can give us temporary peace or serenity, God gives us the permanent peace of a secure relationship with Him. Depending on Him as we do our daily work of preparing meals, caring for children, running errands, or meeting deadlines at the office allows Him to comfort and help us. Are you still expecting peace from the world or enjoying peace from God?

Guarded by Peace

*Do not be anxious about anything, but in every
situation, by prayer and petition, with thanksgiving,
present your requests to God. And the peace of God,
which transcends all understanding, will guard
your hearts and your minds in Christ Jesus.*
PHILIPPIANS 4:6–7 NIV

A pastor's wife consulted a counselor because
she had lost respect for her husband. Due to his
discouragement over difficulties in the church, it
seemed like he no longer walked with God. The
counselor listened to her tearful complaints and
then asked several questions.

Counselor: Do you think your husband will
never be committed to God again? Has he turned
his back on God for good?

Wife: No, I think. . .I hope this is temporary.
If things settle down at church, he will get his
spark back.

Counselor: What do you think God wants you to do to encourage and help your husband?

Wife: Pray for him. Sympathize. Appreciate what I can, and stop pointing out his faults.

Counselor: That's right. You can't fix him— don't try to be his Holy Spirit. Now, let's work on you. You've counseled women who are worried and anxious—what do you tell them?

Wife: I use Philippians 4:6–7 and have them write down every concern they have. Then I tell them to pray over the list, thanking God for what He wants to do. Every time they feel anxious, they should pray over their list again.

Counselor: What will result?

Wife: God's peace will guard their hearts (emotions), and their minds (attitudes) in a way that they will not be able to understand or explain.

The wife took her own advice and experienced God's peace, while her husband eventually found his spiritual footing again.

Four Pieces of Peace

Let the peace of Christ rule in your hearts,
since as members of one body you were
called to peace. And be thankful.

COLOSSIANS 3:15 NIV

Peace has at least four aspects. The first two reflect a peace we inherit because of what God has done for us. The last two are part of our everyday spiritual walk, a peace that we keep with God's help.

1. Accepting the salvation provided by Jesus gives us peace with God (Romans 5:1). We are no longer His enemy; we are His child.
2. All Christians who have peace with God also have peace with each other, because Jesus' death reconciled Jews and Gentiles into one body of believers called *the Church* (Ephesians 2:11–22).

3. Although God provided peace for believers, He tells us to "make every effort to keep the unity of the Spirit through the bond of peace" (Ephesians 4:3 NIV). How? By being "humble and gentle. . .patient, bearing with one another in love" (Ephesians 4:2 NIV). He wants us to have peace in our relationships.

4. We also have peace within ourselves when we practice the disciplines of Philippians 4:6–9. This is the peace Jesus promised to His disciples, even when they suffer (John 16:33). It overcomes a troubled and fearful heart (John 14:1, 27).

Peaceful fellowship with other Christians and inner peace from trusting God to take care of our problems—that's what peace as a fruit of the Spirit looks like.

Be thankful that Jesus' death and resurrection gave us peace with God and with all believers. Ask God to help you live in peace with others and to have a peaceful heart in trusting Him.

Antithesis to Psalm 23

May the God of peace, who. . .brought back from the
dead our Lord Jesus, that great Shepherd of the sheep,
equip you with everything good for doing his will,
and may he work in us what is pleasing to him, through
Jesus Christ, to whom be glory for ever and ever. Amen.
HEBREWS 13:20–22 NIV

The clock is my dictator, I shall not rest. It makes me lie down only when exhausted. It leads me to deep depression. It hounds my soul. It leads me in circles of frenzy for activity's sake. Even though I run frantically from task to task, I will never get it all done, for my 'ideal' is with me. Deadlines and my need for approval, they drive me. They anoint my head with migraines. My in-box overflows. Surely fatigue and time pressure shall follow me all the days of my life, and I will dwell in the bonds of frustration forever."[9]

This sounds like us sometimes, doesn't it? We need the God of peace to sanctify us and work in our spirits, souls, and bodies to keep us from coming apart. Occasionally Jesus also experienced overload from internal and external pressures. "He offered up both prayers and supplications with loud crying and tears. . .and He was heard because of His piety. Although He was a Son, He learned obedience from the things which He suffered (Hebrews 5:7–8 NASB). God's goal for each of us is Christlikeness. So when we cry loudly, weep, and suffer—when life becomes chaotic—remember that Christ will help us to humbly submit and obey as He did. Then, instead of being frenzied and frustrated, the peace of Christ will rule in our hearts (Colossians 3:15 NIV).

Promoting Peace

So then we pursue the things which make
for peace and the building up of one another.
ROMANS 14:19 NASB

Carol's friends Barry and Barb were considering divorce. "I never should have married him in the first place," Barb insisted.

Barry agreed. "We married for the wrong reasons, and now have very little in common. We both deserve something better."

Carol silently prayed for wisdom. Then she asked them to consider God's perspective. "God uses problems to develop and strengthen us. He can redeem even our mistakes and use them for His glory. He is more concerned with our character than with our comfort. His goal is not to make us happy all the time, but to make us more like Christ." Carol challenged them to go home and take two pieces of paper. "On one write all the reasons why you think you should divorce; on the other, reasons to stay together."

Barry and Barb took Carol's advice and made the lists. The next time they met, they told Carol they had decided to work on their problems rather than try to escape, taking their problems with them. In writing the lists, they had opened up and started communicating again.[10]

Carol had been a Proverbs 12:20 "counselor of peace" for Barry and Barb. She rejoiced with them for seeking God in their circumstances rather than living by their own resources. As Barry and Barb stopped pursuing what they thought would be greener grass and began cultivating their marriage, it became the peaceful pasture they hoped for. Working at marriage makes marriage work.

Be Still = Stop Striving

He makes wars cease to the end of the earth;
He breaks the bow and cuts the spear in two. . . .
Be still, and know that I am God; I will be exalted
among the nations, I will be exalted in the earth!
PSALM 46:9–10 NKJV

What does it mean to be still and know God? Some claim that if we stay quiet before God, He will reveal things to us. But this verse exhorts us to be at peace and let God work, not to be contemplative and let God speak. God is our refuge and strength (Psalm 46:1), so we can stop striving, rest, and know that He will be our God who fights our battles.

Psalm 4:4 contains a different Hebrew word translated "be still": "Meditate within your heart on your bed, and be still" (NKJV). This word means "be quiet, rest, wait." The lesson of both verses is to quietly rest in God during distress and conflict; then He will work things out. Both these Hebrew words appear in Psalm 37:7–8: "*Rest* in the LORD and wait patiently for Him; do not fret. . . . *Cease* from anger, and forsake wrath; do not fret" (NKJV). The word *rest* is the same word for "be still" in Psalm 4:4. The word *cease* is the same word for "be still" in Psalm 46:10. Both words imply the opposite of fretting.

Let's apply Psalm 46:10 properly. In the midst of wars and troubles, we should be at peace and stop trying to work everything out ourselves. Because the Lord of hosts is with us (Psalm 46:7, 11) we can rest in Him. When we stop striving, God strives for us. Be still and know it.

Patience Yields Peace

The secret of patience is doing something else in the meantime.

THE SPEAKER'S QUOTE BOOK, ED. ROY B. ZUCK

What Are You Waiting For?

I would have despaired unless I had believed that I would see the goodness of the LORD in the land of the living. Wait for the LORD; be strong and let your heart take courage; yes, wait for the LORD.
PSALM 27:13–14 NASB

How do you react when the light turns yellow as you approach an intersection? A victim of what my friend calls, "the maximum wait," you must sit through the entire red light, especially difficult when you're running late. Yet you cannot move until the light changes—you must wait.

Patience requires waiting, but waiting does not guarantee patience. We can grind out negative thoughts and words while waiting. (Perhaps like me, you have shouted at the light as if it could hear and change its mind.) Or we can wait productively by reviewing memory verses, singing, or praying. Waiting patiently means distracting ourselves from the pain.

But waiting on the Lord means more than being productive until something changes. Am I waiting for God to do what I want or what He wants? Am I waiting until God transforms the person hurting me or until God changes me? Am I waiting for God to satisfy me or sanctify me? God waits, too. "Therefore the LORD *longs* to be gracious to you, and therefore He *waits* on high to have compassion on you. For the LORD is a God of justice; how blessed are all those who *long* for Him" (Isaiah 30:18 NASB). The three italicized words are the same Hebrew word, which means "to wait for or long for." We wait on the Lord with the Holy Spirit's patience when we long for God's gracious compassion and justice. His way, not ours.

A Backward Look

Therefore be patient, brethren, until the coming of the Lord. See how the farmer waits for the precious fruit of the earth, waiting patiently for it until it receives the early and latter rain. You also be patient. Establish your hearts, for the coming of the Lord is at hand.
JAMES 5:7–8 NKJV

Slenderette bush beans are the variety that grows best in our Utah soil. This summer I picked a record number of sixty-two beans from one plant! Often when I'm halfway finished harvesting a row, I'll stretch my aching back and look up to see how far I need to go. *Oh no, I still have half the row left.* But when I look behind me, I see that I've come a long way. I'm actually halfway finished. It all depends on my perspective.

Spiritual patience gives us a proper focus. Instead of wondering when this trial will ever end, we can look back and view how much we have learned and marvel at the strength God has supplied. Patience also makes us look back at

Jesus. How did He handle circumstances similar to ours? He sympathizes with our weaknesses, because He was tempted in every way, yet He never gave in. So He can help us. Like Him, we should learn obedience through our suffering.

All our trials have purpose. God does not waste them. What we endure patiently will sanctify us and develop our character. But God will also enable us to help others who suffer as we have suffered (2 Corinthians 1:1–11). What problem are you facing right now? Look back at what God has done so far. Then ask Him to give you patience until He has harvested all the "produce" He intends for this trial to produce.

A Patient Patient

But those who wait on the Lord shall renew their strength;
they shall mount up with wings like eagles, they shall run
and not be weary, they shall walk and not faint.
Isaiah 40:31 NKJV

There must be a reason why someone who is ill or injured is called a patient. She must be patient while waiting to see a doctor, waiting for test results, and waiting for treatments to work. Our bodies generally heal from surgery and broken bones in six weeks. That makes all the forty-day periods in scripture significant, doesn't it?

I'm learning to be patient while wearing two wrist braces due to a fall that broke both my arms. Every activity takes longer, including typing this book. And yes, God is helping me field-test some of the principles I'm writing about.

"But patience is more than passive waiting," says Pastor Steve Cornell. "It is active restraint that rests in God."[11] While we wait for our bodies to heal, babies to be born and then launched,

dreams and goals to be realized—or not—
finances to improve, warriors to come home, we
must restrain our natural impulses: those cravings
to give in to anger, complaining, and rebellion.
Perhaps that is why we hate to wait. Because it
requires self-restraint.

When we walk in the Spirit, He gives us power
to resist our negative impulses and grow the fruit
of patience. Whether it takes forty minutes, forty
days, forty weeks, or forty years. How actively are
you waiting on God?

A Patient Perspective

"And he who does not take his cross and follow after Me is not worthy of Me. He who finds his life will lose it, and he who loses his life for My sake will find it."
Matthew 10:38–39 NKJV

Marie suffers from rheumatoid arthritis among other things. Consequently her fingers lock up if she doesn't inject herself with a chemo drug twice a week. The drug makes her sick and debilitated for six to eight hours, so she plans her schedule accordingly. Marie tries to see this from God's perspective.

She says, "This is not my 'cross to bear.' My cross is what every Christian is called to bear—the cross of discipleship. That means spending our lives pursuing God instead of wasting it on things concerned only with this world. RA is not my cross—it's God's calling for me. God made my body the way it is, so evidently these disabilities will be how I can best glorify Him. My suffering has God-intended benefits. Instead of crying for its removal, I must cry out for God to complete His work in me."

The fruit of the Spirit is evident in Marie's life. She suffers cheerfully and patiently, because she sees it as her calling from God.

Are you following Christ by living for Him each day instead of for yourself? If so, you are bearing the cross of discipleship. When it comes to the limitations of your health and body, or circumstances you cannot change, or unexpected losses, have you accepted them as God's calling for you? If so, God will give you the patience you need to live cheerfully in dependence on Him.[12]

Trust Issues

Therefore humble yourselves under the mighty hand of God, that He may exalt you in due time, casting all your care upon Him, for He cares for you.
1 Peter 5:6–7 nkjv

$\mathcal{P}$atience does not *ignore* offenses or obstacles, temptations or trials. It *endures* them without complaint and without anxiety. "Patience is not the same as indifference," states Oswald Chambers. "Patience conveys the idea of someone who is tremendously strong and able to withstand all assaults."[13] But the strength to endure without anxiety is not self-conjured. It comes from casting our cares on the One who cares for us. Not only is worry unnecessary for a Christian, it is disrespectful of God. It says He is not trustworthy, not capable of taking care of us; He is not enough. Spirit-filled Christians counteract those lies with truth.

Do you have trust issues? Wounds from the

past often condition us to protect ourselves from further hurts, so we emotionally decide that we can't trust anyone. Projecting this attitude onto God results in anxiety and impatience. I admit, when God doesn't meet my expectations, I tend to question, complain, and nag Him rather than rest in Him. I need patience, even with God! Journeying with God is a process of discovery. The more we know who God is, the more we will trust that everything He does is for our growth, others' good, and His glory. The better we know Him, the easier it is to humbly accept His plan, cast on Him our cares, and live patiently in His strength.[14]

Need a Longer Temper?

*And we urge you, brothers and sisters, warn those
who are idle and disruptive, encourage the disheartened,
help the weak, be patient with everyone.*
1 Thessalonians 5:14 niv

Can we really be patient with everyone? With
a screaming and kicking two-year-old? With
ear-bud-plugged teens who can't look up from
their phones? With a husband who throws dirty
clothes on the floor as if you were a maid? With
the coworker who schmoozes the boss? With
the sister who won't take her turn cleaning for
your elderly parents? We all could be patient if it
weren't for people!

We have no problem being patient with
those who don't irritate or inconvenience us. But
God says *everyone*. Of course, this is not possible
without God's Spirit as our helper. He enables
us to control our natural (sinful) impulses and
obey what God wants. In the verses following
1 Thessalonians 5:14, He tells us how to have

patience with everyone: don't repay evil with evil; seek what is good; rejoice always; pray always; and give thanks in everything, for these things are God's will for us.

The word *patience* means "long-tempered" or "long-suffering." It is part of God's nature, and He wants to develop it in us, too. But it takes patience to develop patience—it's a process. Colossians 1:11 is part of a prayer where Paul asks God to strengthen believers "with all power, according to His glorious might, for the attaining of all steadfastness and patience; joyously" (NASB). Do you need a longer temper? Ask God for His strength to help you become long-tempered with everyone.

Examples of Patience

*Brothers and sisters, as an example of patience
in the face of suffering, take the prophets
who spoke in the name of the Lord.*
JAMES 5:10 NIV

A new gadget or appliance used to come with
an instruction manual. As technology became
more complex, manuals grew to hundreds of
pages. Things have changed. I have Bible research
software that includes a library of 775 resources.
The entire package came in two CDs—one for
installation and one for the product. Instead of a
hefty manual, it gives video tutorials.

We used to think of the Bible as our
instruction manual for life, which it is. But in
contemporary thought, it can be our tutorial. It
was written for our instruction so that we would
have hope. That hope comes through endurance
and comfort we receive from the scriptures
(Romans 15:4). The biblical people who endured

now live in eternity with their hope fulfilled. We can endure as they did through our many life experiences that test our patience. By studying their lives we learn how God worked with them and through them. The good and bad events in their lives tutor us to respond to everything we face with dependence on our trustworthy God. Then the patience we need will mature in us gradually, like apples on a tree.

The prophets learned to suffer patiently, especially when the people they ministered to rejected their message and mistreated them. Likewise, we can learn to have the fruit of patience with difficult people and adverse circumstances. Do you want to be more patient? Then access the *Tutorial*.

The Patience of Job

We count those blessed who endured. You have heard of the endurance of Job and have seen the outcome of the Lord's dealings, that the Lord is full of compassion and is merciful.

JAMES 5:11 NASB

A four-letter word for patience is *w-a-i-t*. Waiting on God does not come naturally. It comes supernaturally, and sometimes God helps it along by sending problems. That's why Job is known for his patience. He had to wait for his sores to heal, his grief to process, his friends to go home, his barns to be rebuilt, and for God to show up. The book of Job is not about why the righteous suffer. It is about God being worthy of our love and trust and service, even when He allows us to suffer. God is worth living for, suffering for, dying for, because He is our God, not because it benefits or blesses us.

Job had begged for God to answer him, but instead God came with about seventy questions, including this one: "Will the faultfinder contend with the Almighty? Let him who reproves God answer it" (Job 40:2 NASB). Job had asked "Why," when he should have asked "Who?"

Job replied to God's questions, "Behold, I am insignificant; what can I reply to You? I lay my hand on my mouth" (Job 40:4 NASB). Job was willing to rest his case in the hands of an infinite God, who is always good, but also unpredictable. We are too finite to figure Him out. He knows what He's doing in our lives, and that means we don't have to. We can wait for Him to do what is best for us. Job's job, and ours, is to trust God no matter what.

Patience with Problems

Being strengthened with all power according to his glorious might so that you may have great endurance and patience. . .
COLOSSIANS 1:11 NIV

During times of difficulty, do you need a prayer buddy? Will the Holy Spirit do? Consider Romans 8:26, "In the same way, the Spirit helps us in our weakness. We do not know what we ought to pray for, but the Spirit himself intercedes for us through wordless groans" (NIV). And Jesus also promises to appeal to the Father for us: "Christ Jesus. . .is at the right hand of God and is also interceding for us" (Romans 8:34 NIV).

However, their requests might be different from ours. We say, "Lord, please remove this obstacle," while they seek to redeem it. We pray for God to change our circumstances or the people hurting us, but they want to change us. We say, "Show me why You are doing this," while they say, "Show her who God is." God is more interested in developing us than in delivering us, so He makes us patient through difficulties.

He wants to work in us through the husband we have, or through the children He has gifted to us—perhaps even children with special needs—or through having no children. He uses health problems and disabilities; financial limitations; where we live, even if we don't like living there; unmet needs; unreached goals; and unfulfilled dreams, because He wants us to find our sufficiency in Him (2 Corinthians 3:5).

Knowing that Jesus and the Holy Spirit pray for us can strengthen us to patiently endure. God will answer their prayers.

Kindness NEEDS
SELF-CONTROL

*Kindness always pays, but it pays
most when you don't do it for pay.*

THE SPEAKER'S QUOTE BOOK, ED. ROY B. ZUCK

A Mother's Kindness

Just as a nursing mother cares for her children, so we cared for you. Because we loved you so much, we were delighted to share with you not only the gospel of God but our lives as well.
1 THESSALONIANS 2:7–8 NIV

We picture kindness as a mother's touch on her feverish child's head or the careful way a dad holds his newborn baby so her head does not wobble. Paul felt that way about the church at Thessalonica. He nurtured them, met their needs, and treated them kindly so he would not be a burden to them. As an apostle, he could have asked, or demanded, that they serve him. Instead Paul supported himself while living there. It pleased him to share his life with them.

If you had a good mother, you know what it means to be self-sacrificing. She gave up sleep to nurse newborn you, put her aspirations aside to nurture yours, and probably even ate the turkey wings at Thanksgiving so you could have the meatier parts. This does not mean she indulged you or fixed all your problems. She no doubt taught you about delayed gratification, let you experience consequences for your choices, and insisted that you follow through on your commitments. Kindness produced by the Spirit does not allow people to take advantage of us. It gives us the right attitude of putting others before ourselves.

When we focus on serving people and meeting their needs, we will treat them kindly like a good mother does with her children. The Holy Spirit will empower us to respond with kind actions and words, even when people seem childish or ungrateful.

Biblical Kindness

*"The LORD bless him!" Naomi said to her
daughter-in-law. "He has not stopped showing
his kindness to the living and the dead."*
RUTH 2:20 NIV

In Israel's history, the time of the judges was
characterized by spiritual and moral decay. Enter
Ruth, an example of kindness. The Hebrew
word *hesed* applies to the Lord in Ruth 1:8 and
Ruth 2:20, and to Ruth in Ruth 3:10. *Hesed* has
no English parallel, so we translate it as "loving-
kindness" or "loyal love." Ruth extended hesed-
kindness to her mother-in-law, Naomi. It was not
conditioned on Naomi's responses. By her own
admission Naomi felt empty and bitter because
she had buried her husband and both sons (1:11–
13). But Ruth, also a widow, gave up her homeland
and relatives in Moab, embraced Yahweh as her
God, and promised to spend the rest of her life
with Naomi (Ruth 1:15–17).

After telling Naomi that she was committed

to her, Ruth asked Naomi's permission to provide food for her (Ruth 2:2). Sometimes we think of ways to help others and dump it on them whether they want help or not. But kindness means meeting someone's felt needs with their permission. Ruth's actions began to have a positive effect on Naomi. She started seeing God's kindness and hope for a future (Ruth 2:19–20). Then Naomi thought of an idea that must have sounded crazy, but Ruth respected Naomi by doing it (Ruth 3:3–5). Through Ruth's commitment to Naomi, her practical help, and her obedience to Naomi's ideas, Ruth nurtured Naomi until she regained her ability to nurture others (Ruth 4:16).[15] Let's follow Ruth's example of kindness.

Controlled by Kindness

When he went ashore he saw a great crowd, and he had compassion on them and healed their sick.
MATTHEW 14:14 ESV

Most of us are good at multitasking. We can manage duties and diapers, people and papers, recipes and receipts—all simultaneously. Usually. Except for mornings when the dog throws up on the carpet, you get the kids to school late, your mother asks a favor, and the boss gives you something to do "before you leave today." So much for your plans to work out on your lunch break. Some days run smoothly, but other days we run with the bulls or simply run in place and go nowhere. Does the fruit of the Spirit cover those inevitable intrusions that knock us off course? What did Jesus do with interruptions?

After Jesus' hometown had rejected Him, and He learned that His cousin and supporter, John the Baptist, had been beheaded, He sailed to a solitary place with His disciples. However, a large, needy crowd disrupted His plans. Despite His own hurts, He responded to the hurting multitudes with compassion and kindness.

When our to-do list gets out of control, Jesus understands. He saw interruptions as opportunities to minister. Yes, we do need time to refresh ourselves, and Jesus took that time. After He fed the multitudes and sent them home, He went up a mountain alone to pray (Matthew 14:23). But He didn't let hard circumstances control His attitude. When His plans got knocked over, kindness spilled out. By depending on Him, we can respond in kind.[16]

Kindness Makes Relationships Grow

Let all bitterness, wrath, anger, clamor, and evil
speaking be put away from you, with all malice.
And be kind to one another, tenderhearted, forgiving
one another, even as God in Christ forgave you.
EPHESIANS 4:31–32 NKJV

"Be kind to your wife" is how a pastor in
Wisconsin closes his phone conversations to
friends. Following his simple recommendation
lends harmony to relationships. As a fellow pastor,
my husband includes Ephesians 4:32 in wedding
ceremonies. Kindness is like plant food to all our
relationships, whether with husband and relatives;
friends and coworkers; or to checkers, servers,
phone agents, and salesclerks. Kind words and
deeds minimize conflicts and nurture our bonds.
By the same token, tenderheartedness waters our
relationships. They dry up when we fail to be

sensitive to each other's feelings or empathize with others.

Along with kindness and tenderness, we must also forgive offenses. This kills the noxious weeds of bitterness and malice. We forgive because God commands it, not because the offender deserves it. Do we dare hold a grudge against someone when God has forgiven all our offenses against Him? When we trust in Christ for eternal life, His blood cleanses us from all sin and provides open fellowship with God through Christ. Likewise, forgiving one another keeps our human relationships open and eliminates feelings of resentment.

Ephesians also says to put away anger and evil speaking. Ephesians 4:29 tells us how—our words should build up and give grace to those who hear. The fruit of the Spirit includes words of encouragement spoken graciously. Would you like your relationships to grow? Nourish them with Ephesians 4:32 principles.

Kind Words

She opens her mouth with wisdom,
and the teaching of kindness is on her tongue.
PROVERBS 31:26 ESV

Sometimes we women are teased for having well-developed verbal skills. Of course, usually the strong, silent type of men do the teasing! Stereotypes aside, when God included in the wisdom literature of the Bible a chapter about a woman of virtue, He mentioned her hands (or palms) in seven out of twenty-two verses, and her mouth in only one verse. God says her mouth disperses wisdom and teaches kindness—the same word often translated "loving-kindness" in the Hebrew scriptures.

When kindness characterizes us, we will not only do kind deeds, we will speak kind words and control our tone of voice. We often speak soft, gentle words to a cute little baby, but let him reach the potty-training stage, and what tone comes out of our mouths? (I speak from experience.) Have you conditioned your preteen to respond and obey only when your request reaches a certain decibel? Or perhaps your husband has messed up big time and you are yelling at him when your cell phone goes off. You press the button and sweetly say, "Hello?"

Yes, we can control how we talk. We can unlearn bad habits and practice speaking kind words with a kind voice, but not without the Holy Spirit's help. Submit your mouth to the Lord every day, asking Him to set a guard over both what you say and the way you say it (Psalm 141:3).

Put on Kindness

So, as those who have been chosen of God, holy and
beloved, put on a heart of compassion, kindness,
humility, gentleness and patience; bearing with
one another, and forgiving each other.
COLOSSIANS 3:12–13 NASB

Every stage of life challenges us to greater
dependence on God. The financial struggles of
young adulthood may be followed by parenting
preschoolers. Don't worry—that stage ends,
but now you have teens and their hormones to
navigate. While raising teens, you may join the
"sandwich generation" if your aging parents also
need your care. Add a hot flash or two, or twenty
every day. (At least PMS has ended.) Some women
even raise grandkids. Does life ever get easy? No,
but Colossians 3:12–13 tells us to "wear" kindness,
patience, and forgiveness so we will reflect God's
holiness and love to others.

Eventually failing health gets added to our

experiences. Life is a series of struggles punctuated by periods of peace. Much as we'd like, we will never have heaven on earth. Aren't you glad God is sufficient for all our serving: "Not that we are adequate in ourselves. . .but our adequacy is from God" (2 Corinthians 3:5 NASB). For our finances: "God loves a cheerful giver. And God is able to make all grace abound to you, so that always having all sufficiency in everything, you may have an abundance for every good deed" (2 Corinthians 9:7–8 NASB). And for all our suffering: "'My grace is sufficient for you, for power is perfected in weakness. . . . For when I am weak, then I am strong'" (2 Corinthians 12:9–10 NASB).

Memorize these passages about God's sufficiency so you can enjoy each stage of life in fellowship with Him.

Kindness Cures
Feeling Useless

Love is kind and is not jealous;
love does not brag and is not arrogant.
1 CORINTHIANS 13:4 NASB

The purpose of fruit is to be picked and consumed. The Holy Spirit grows His fruit in us so we can nourish others. We aren't thinking about our own benefit, and yet, showing love and kindness to others blesses us as well. Healing others helps us to heal ourselves. Perhaps no one knows this better than people who have lost their spouses.[17] They share a unique bond, even if their mate's death was expected. Being widowed results in a sudden loss of identity, companionship, and intimacy, among other things.

Most widows say that confusion and decision-making overwhelm them at first. They struggle to adjust to being single and lonely, shouldering their late husband's previous responsibilities, dealing with his possessions, and sometimes parenting children who are also grieving. Like it or not, they must reinvent a new life for themselves. It takes time for widows to find their footing and stabilize emotionally. Many claim that happens best when they reach out to other needy people. Extending kindness to someone in need lets them momentarily forget their own losses.

Everyone needs to be needed. Whether widowed, divorced, single, or married, when we do kind things for others, we make our own life more meaningful and give it purpose. Think of someone you know who could use a kind word or a helping hand. What will you do for that person this week?

Generosity Has Built-In Rewards

The wicked borrow and do not repay,
but the righteous give generously.
PSALM 37:21 NIV

You will never regret being generous. The Spirit's fruit of kindness often involves not only our time, but also our money or services. Part of being kind to others is giving to them with no expectation of them giving back. And yet there is a payback—we get personal satisfaction when we help others. Proverbs 11:24–25 says: "One person gives freely, yet gains even more; another withholds unduly, but comes to poverty. A generous person will prosper; whoever refreshes others will be refreshed" (NIV). We may regret that we didn't give more, and we may feel bad when someone takes advantage of our generosity, but we won't be sorry that we did the best we could with what we had at the time.

Jesus taught, "Give, and it will be given to you. A good measure, pressed down, shaken together and running over, will be poured into your lap. For with the measure you use, it will be measured to you" (Luke 6:38 NIV). He encouraged His followers to lay up treasure in heaven, not earth (Matthew 6:19–21), to train their eyes away from covetousness and greed (Matthew 6:22–23), and to serve God not money (Matthew 6:24). We will have these right attitudes toward money when we use it to minister to others.

Ask God to help you stay centered on what you can give not what you can get. You may have empty pockets, but you will be full of kindness.

God Is Kind

*But when the kindness and love of God our Savior
appeared, he saved us, not because of righteous
things we had done, but because of his mercy.*
TITUS 3:4–5 NIV

Satan has captured us and put us on a train to the death camp. This is our human condition—we belong to Satan. "The one who practices sin is of the devil" (1 John 3:8 NASB). We may not know the train's destination, but as sinners, we have been condemned to death (Romans 6:23).

But Jesus boards Satan's train. He announces that anyone who wants to get off and come over to His eternal-life train may do so. "The one who comes to Me I will certainly not cast out" (John 6:37 NASB). Someone replies, "But I don't have a ticket. How much does it cost?"

Jesus answers, "It cost me my life, but I paid in full for your ticket. Will you take it and live forever with me?"

For Jesus' train we don't have to be worthy or even pay part of the fare. We simply depend on Jesus to save us from spiritual death by believing what He said: "Truly, truly, I say to you, he who hears My word, and believes Him who sent Me, has eternal life, and does not come into judgment, but has passed out of death into life" (John 5:24 NASB).

Ephesians 2:7–8 tells us about God's kindness in saving us from our sins: "He might show the surpassing riches of His grace in kindness toward us in Christ Jesus. For by grace you have been saved through faith; and that not of yourselves, it is the gift of God" (NASB). The ticket is free because Jesus bought it with His life.

Which train are you on?

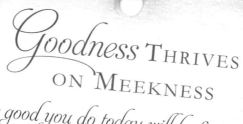

Goodness Thrives on Meekness

The good you do today will be forgotten tomorrow. Do good anyway.

GARY C. GRIESSNER

Suffering for Doing Good

But if you suffer for doing good and you endure it,
this is commendable before God.
1 PETER 2:20 NIV

We often think goodness will always be rewarded.
It will not. Sometimes goodness causes suffering.
Ask any whistle-blower. Ask the mother of a
prodigal child. Ask anyone who's been persecuted
for her testimony. No, goodness is not always
rewarded in this life. But God views it differently.
Suffering for doing what is right honors Him. This
kind of goodness requires courage and conviction,
spiritual strength and moral stamina. In short, it
takes dependence on God.

Even though we may suffer for doing good,
1 Peter 2:12 tell us to do good anyway. "Live such
good lives among the pagans that, though they
accuse you of doing wrong, they may see your
good deeds and glorify God" (NIV). Eventually
their foolish talk will be silenced (1 Peter 2:15),
and they may even regret slandering your good

behavior (1 Peter 3:16). Either way, the only opinion we need to be concerned with is God's, our righteous and impartial Judge (1 Peter 1:17). Someday He will make everything right.

Jesus Christ is our example of unjust suffering. How did He handle it? "When they hurled their insults at him, he did not retaliate; when he suffered, he made no threats. Instead, he entrusted himself to him who judges justly" (1 Peter 2:23 NIV). We can do the same, as 1 Peter 4:19 exhorts: "So then, those who suffer according to God's will should commit themselves to their faithful Creator and continue to do good" (NIV).

Win-Win

For we are His workmanship, created in
Christ Jesus for good works, which God prepared
beforehand so that we would walk in them.
EPHESIANS 2:10 NASB

What is the difference between being good and doing good? None of us can be good on our own because we are born sinners. We inherited sin from our first father, Adam (Romans 3:10–12; 5:12). We are also sinners because we sin (Romans 3:13). It's a lose-lose situation.

Fortunately we have a good God. He provided the way to declare us righteous. Jesus paid the penalty for our sin when He died in our place. (Read Romans 5.) When we trust in Christ by faith, we get His goodness, righteousness, as a free gift. To show our gratitude for *being good* in God's eyes, we want to please Him by *doing good*. As if all that is not enough, God enables us to do good by making it part of the Spirit's fruit.

Remember, doing good works does not *earn* our salvation, it does not *prove* we belong to God, and it does not *reimburse* Him in any way. We work for Him out of appreciation for His free gifts. Like the college student who worked hard to make the dean's list after her dad bought her a car because she knew it would please him. But wait! There's more! Second Timothy 3:16–17 says that scripture thoroughly equips us for every good work, and 2 Corinthians 3:5–6 says God will make us adequate as His servants. God not only prepared us for good works, He enables us to do them—a win-win combination.

Not Showing Off Myself

Do nothing out of selfish ambition or vain conceit. Rather, in humility value others above yourselves, not looking to your own interests but each of you to the interests of the others.
PHILIPPIANS 2:3–4 NIV

Goodness produced by the Spirit enables us to put others first, shine the spotlight on someone else and off ourselves. It helps us become more concerned about listening than talking, about making others feel good about themselves.

This can be a struggle when we seek others' approval above God's. Take Lucy for example. As the baby of her family, Lucy was indulged in childhood. Her siblings catered to her, and she was the darling of her parents. In adulthood she had to learn to keep quiet when tempted to boast about herself. Instead, she now evaluates her motives by asking herself, *Am I doing this for attention or for God?*

Lucy says, "When my focus is on myself, I wrongly think that I deserve more from God. It took me a while to learn that God owes me nothing! I grew up with this false sense of entitlement, and one day I realized that I expected God to do what I wanted. Now I try to remember that everything I have is an undeserved gift. God gives generously, not because He sees something good in me, but simply because He is good. That motivates me to do good things to please Him."

Lucy still struggles with self-indulgence and a craving for approval from others, but she asks God to help her stay in the background and put others ahead of herself. God's approval is what counts.

A Good Deed Daily

She does him good and not evil all the days of her life.
PROVERBS 31:12 NASB

Proverbs 31 seems unattainable until we make two observations:

1. Being virtuous means developing a life-long skill that will benefit our family, the needy (Proverbs 31:20), and ultimately the community (Proverbs 31:24). For the Proverbs 31 woman it was making garments. For Ruth—the only biblical woman called virtuous—it was caring for her mother-in-law.

2. See the passage as a photo album of a woman's entire life, not a log of her day. In fact, the only thing she does every day is something good for her husband. Married women who are virtuous need that focus.

However, doing good is a biblical theme for all Christians. We are to be fruitful in every good work (Colossians 1:10) and ready to do whatever is good (Titus 3:1). God equips us for every good thing to do His will (Hebrews 13:20–21). He saved us by faith, not by our works, so we will walk in good works afterward (Ephesians 2:8–10). Second Timothy 2:21 compares us to vessels God wants to use and says that if we cleanse ourselves, we will be "sanctified, useful to the Master, prepared for every good work" (NASB). Galatians 6:10 tells us to do good to all people, especially to other Christians, as we have opportunity.

What good can you do for another person today? Mentally put yourself in her stilettos, sneakers, or sandals, and consider what you could do that she would appreciate. Ask God for discernment and wisdom; then go and do something good.

Women's Work

*[She] is well known for her good deeds, such as bringing
up children, showing hospitality, washing the feet of
the Lord's people, helping those in trouble and
devoting herself to all kinds of good deeds.*
1 TIMOTHY 5:10 NIV

*G*od talks about widows who deserve to be
supported by the local church if they have no
other source of support. He designates this
benefit for widows who are known for good
works. Even if you aren't a widow, God's standard
for women includes devotion to good deeds.
First Timothy lists several examples: "brought up
children. . .shown hospitality to strangers. . .
washed the saints' feet. . .assisted those in distress"
(NASB).

What—no self-development? Not "being the
best you can be"? 'Fraid not. Goodness produced
by the Holy Spirit involves helping others. This
includes meeting children's needs (In what ways

do you help children?); having people over (Have you prepared a meal for guests or taken someone out to eat recently?); serving others in lowly tasks (What behind-the-scene jobs do you do without pay or recognition?); and caring for people who are suffering (Do you do more than pray for them?).

What if you are not a widow? All widows are women, so this list must be commendable things all women should involve themselves in—not by self-effort or with a "martyr complex," but by our fellowship with God. First Timothy 2:9–10 tells us to dress ourselves "by means of good works, as is proper for women making a claim to godliness" (NASB). Finally, Titus 2:3–5 tells older women to teach younger women to be good.

God can help us learn how to be good to others with the time and resources we have. This kind of goodness is what God wants in His women.

Goodness Is Contagious

Beloved, do not imitate evil but imitate good. Whoever does
good is from God; whoever does evil has not seen God.
3 JOHN 11 ESV

Experiencing God's goodness motivates and
empowers us to do good instead of evil. When
we treat others with goodness and charity, they
will often return the favor. The Spirit's fruit is
contagious like that. Perhaps that is why Paul told
believers to imitate him just as he imitated Christ
(1 Corinthians 11:1; 4:14–16; 2 Thessalonians 3:7–
9). We can learn goodness from other Christians.

When you think of a "good person," who
comes to your mind? What makes her good?
Should you copy some of her practices? Yet
3 John 11 implies more than imitating good
behavior. We can do good externally with evil
motives internally, such as seeking approval for
our ego's sake. Some Christians follow their
pastor's standards in order to please him, instead
of considering what would please God.

Ultimately our actions should reflect fruit that the Lord wants from us, as Ephesians 5:9–10 states: "For the fruit of the Light consists in all goodness and righteousness and truth, trying to learn what is pleasing to the Lord" (NASB). We would neglect our family and exhaust ourselves if we tried to take every opportunity to do good things for others, but Galatians 1:10 teaches us to please God, not necessarily people. So we should ask ourselves, "What actions and decisions would most please the Lord? What would be best for me and my family spiritually?" When our good deeds reflect our desire to please God, then others will be able to imitate us.

The Christian's Game Plan

Hate what is evil; cling to what is good. . . .
Overcome evil with good.
ROMANS 12:9, 21 NIV

"Have you ever played the game of Flinch?" a teacher asked her Sunday school class. No one had heard of it. She showed them the Flinch cards, which contained numbers one through fifteen—all the same color. "If we wanted to have fun playing Flinch, what should we do? How should we play?" she asked.

Students suggested several ideas, but eventually someone gave the correct answer: "We have to read the rules."

The teacher then compared this to Christian living: "In playing the game of life, we must follow God's rules."

Romans 12:9–21 lists practical rules for displaying goodness: "Love must be sincere. Hate what is evil; cling to what is good. Be devoted to one another in love. Honor one another above yourselves. . . . Be joyful in hope, patient in affliction, faithful in prayer. Share with the Lord's people who are in need. Practice hospitality. . . . Rejoice with those who rejoice; mourn with those who mourn. Live in harmony with one another. . . . Associate with people of low position. Do not be conceited. . . . Live at peace with everyone. . . . Overcome evil with good" (NIV).

Life can be harmonious when players take turns and follow the rules, but many times they cheat, scatter all the cards, or refuse to play. It is hardest to be good when others don't play nice, but the Holy Spirit helps us to overcome evil with good and to play by God's rules.

The Taste Test

*Oh, taste and see that the L*ORD *is good; blessed is the man*
*who trusts in Him! Oh, fear the L*ORD, *you His saints!*
There is no want to those who fear Him.
PSALM 34:8–9 NKJV

Often we shop to make ourselves feel better.
Buying something new gives a temporary fix to
our feelings of inadequacy or self-pity. We browse
the shelves in hopes of uncovering the perfect
purse or flattering footwear to boost our self-
image. And we sometimes allow other people
to set our self-worth. Isn't that one reason why
we shop—to impress people? If our motive is
approval from others, we may achieve it by our
taste in clothes. But Psalm 34 encourages us to
taste and see God's goodness. That gives us a
higher purpose. When we trust God's goodness,
we don't need perks from the fashion industry to
make us feel loved and accepted.

Psalm 34 also says that those who seek the

Lord lack no good thing (v. 10). This reminds us that spiritual pursuits give permanent satisfaction, while all material goods, on the other hand, will eventually wear out. Fearing God means turning from evil and doing good (vv.11–14). The psalm ends with descriptions of the *righteous*—another word for those who are good. Read Psalm 34 and make two shopping lists: "What God wants me to do" and "What God does for me when I trust Him."

Stuffing our closet with new purchases is fun, but "shopping" for insights about God gives lasting fulfillment and doesn't diminish our bank balance. Indulge yourself in a banquet of God's goodness today.

Be Good to Your Enemies

"But I say to you, love your enemies, bless those who curse you, do good to those who hate you, and pray for those who spitefully use you and persecute you."
MATTHEW 5:44 NKJV

If we respond in kind to those who hurt us, antagonism escalates. But when we repay evil with good, it catches our adversary off guard and defuses the situation. Consider this ironic story in 2 Kings 6. God kept revealing to Elisha the locations where Israel's enemy, the Arameans, would strike. So the king of Aram suspected a traitor in his camp. But his advisers set him straight—Israel had a prophet of God.

Aram's king sent many troops to capture Elisha, which terrified his servant, but Elisha remained calm. First, he asked God to open the servant's eyes to see God's spiritual army surrounding and protecting them. Second, he asked God to close the Arameans' eyes so they could not recognize Elisha. Next, he told the enemy army that he would take them to the man they were seeking. Instead, Elisha took them directly to the king of Israel. Then Elisha asked God to restore their sight. Suddenly they realized they were captives. Israel's king also recognized his incredible opportunity and said, "Shall I kill them?"

Elisha said, "No, feed them."

So the king of Israel prepared a great feast before sending them home. The result? They did not attack Israel again.

Is there an adversary you need to be good to? Your husband's ex-wife? Your mother-in-law? The coworker who wants your job? Pray for them, and ask God to open your eyes to see something good you can do for them.

Faithfulness

REQUIRES FAITH

In every change,
He faithful will remain.

KATHARINA A. VON SCHLEGEL, "BE STILL, MY SOUL"

We Need a
Bird-Brained View

"Look at the birds of the air: they neither sow nor reap nor gather into barns, and yet your heavenly Father feeds them. Are you not of more value than they?"
MATTHEW 6:26 ESV

The more we understand God's faithfulness to us, the more we will desire to remain faithful to Him. A poem I learned in childhood illustrates two birds talking to each other:

> Said the robin to the sparrow,
> "I would really like to know
> Why these anxious human beings
> Rush about and worry so."
>
> Said the sparrow to the robin,
> "Friend, I think that it must be
> That they have no Heavenly Father
> Such as cares for you and me."[18]

The sparrow was confident in God's faithful care, as if it knew what Jesus had said about sparrows. But Jesus was not giving a nature lesson. His point was that if God cares even for sparrows of little worth, how much more does He know and meet our needs, down to the smallest detail, like hairs on our heads. "So do not fear; you are more valuable than many sparrows" (Matthew 10:31 NASB). And we have no excuse for doubting God.

Most of us live with unreached goals and unfulfilled dreams, either because of choices we have made or circumstances forced on us. We can let these longings be catalysts to draw us to God. He knows our needs and our desires, and He invites us to rest under His wings (Psalm 91). He is our wise, loving, powerful, all-sufficient God. We can faithfully trust Him instead of rushing about and worrying. Whenever you feel anxious or overwhelmed, fly to Him.

Considering God Faithful

Now it is required that those who have
been given a trust must prove faithful.
1 CORINTHIANS 4:2 NIV

One of the people of faith in Hebrews 11 is said
to have been faithful to God by believing that "the
One who had promised was faithful" (HCSB). God
did something extraordinary through this person
because God keeps His promises. This enabled
that hero of the faith to trust Him and be faithful,
too. Who was it? Sarah. "And by faith even Sarah,
who was past childbearing age, was enabled to
bear children because she considered him faithful
who had made the promise" (Hebrews 11:11 NIV).

In practical terms, Sarah had at least three
strikes against her. She had never conceived, she
was postmenopausal, and she and Abram already
had what they thought was the "son of promise."
Ishmael had been born thirteen years earlier, after
Sarah gave Hagar to Abram as a second wife

(Genesis 16:3). Then God shook things up and said Sarah would be a ninety-year-old pregnant mother. How did they take the news? Abraham and Sarah both laughed (Genesis 18:10–15). That is how their son Isaac got his name, which means laughter.

Evidently Sarah decided it was better to believe in God for the impossible than to understand Him through logic. After laughing, and denying it, she must have concluded, "If God said it, I believe it." So her portrait hangs in the Hebrews 11 Hall of Faithfulness. Like Sarah, we can faithfully rely on God's promises because He faithfully keeps them. What promise of God in scripture do you need to trust Him for today?

Faithful and Willing

Without faith it is impossible to please Him,
for he who comes to God must believe that He is
and that He is a rewarder of those who seek Him.
HEBREWS 11:6 NASB

Like Sarah, we can show faithfulness because we believe God is faithful to us and to His promises. We may have an impossible boss or a bad habit we cannot break. Perhaps we consider ourselves to be past our prime—too late for God to use us now. But all God requires of His disciples at any age is faithfulness and willingness.

The people God placed in Hebrews 11 are our examples of faithfulness. They believed what God said, and they believed He would reward them for seeking Him. These things please God. It doesn't mean they were above reproach. With the possible exception of Joseph, everyone in the chapter had a major mess-up. Look at Samson. No doubt his spiritual vision sharpened after he lost his physical vision. By the end of his life he must have learned his lesson about pleasing God not himself.

Why do we, along with these people of God, serve and suffer faithfully? Because it pleases God. It glorifies Him. This is motive enough, but amazingly God also rewards those who seek Him and serve Him. No matter how we may have failed God in the past, it is never too late to live for Him now. He probably won't ask you or me to be a ninety-year-old new mother, but He does ask us to be faithful and willing to the end.

Running Our Race

Therefore, since we are surrounded by such a great cloud of witnesses, let us throw off everything that hinders and the sin that so easily entangles. And let us run with perseverance the race marked out for us.
Hebrews 12:1 NIV

The "great cloud of witnesses" in Hebrews 12 have finished their races. Their example can help us evaluate our life of faith. Use the following questions as a checklist for faithfulness:

1. *What key events in my life have evidenced my trust in God?* Abraham would answer, "I obeyed God's inexplicable command and bound my beloved son as a sacrifice" (Hebrews 11:17–19).

2. *When have I experienced complete dependence on God instead of on my own resources?* Moses' mother would say, "When I was not afraid of the king's command. Besides, I did throw my baby in the Nile—I just

put him in a waterproof basket first"
(Hebrews 11:23).

3. *Is my focus on my eventual eternity with God
or on my earthly life?* Moses would say,
"Instead of becoming the next pharaoh,
I chose to suffer with God's people,
because living for God was more valuable
than all the treasures of Egypt" (Hebrews
11:24–26).

4. *Can I point to a time when I have risked
everything for God?* Rahab would reply, "I
put my life on the line when I hid the
spies, because I believed their God was
the true God" (Hebrews 11:31).

What do these people witness to us about?
They testify that a life of faith is worth all the
sacrifices they made and the risks they took. We
can be faithful to the end and endure our life-race
by trusting in God like they did. Write out your
answers to the checklist for faithfulness.

Spiritual Marines

I thank Christ Jesus our Lord, who has strengthened me,
because He considered me faithful, putting me into service.
1 TIMOTHY 1:12 NASB

"When we counsel young people about what to look for in a mate, we fail to mention loyalty," Ray said. "My first wife was gorgeous and intelligent but not loyal to me. We divorced. Then I married Julia forty years ago. She has been faithful and dedicated to me. How I value that."

It's true. American culture has influenced us to believe that change equals progress, and change is good. Thus loyalty is no longer valued. My parents built a home and lived in it all their married lives. My dad worked the same job for forty years. They stayed married even when their relationship faltered. Vows were made to be kept. That kind of faithfulness is becoming rare except in people devoted to God. This does not mean we should never improve our situation or change careers. But it means faithfully doing what God wants even when we'd rather run from commitments or bow to temptation.

With the Holy Spirit's help we can keep trusting God even when life hurts. Although our feelings fluctuate, we can work at our marriage relationships. We can carry out our obligations and keep our promises. (However, this does not mean staying in an abusive relationship.) Cultural peer pressure says, "You don't have to put up with this," but God prizes and rewards faithfulness.

We can be *semper fi* (always faithful), even when it's not popular.

By Faith Not by Sight

For we walk by faith, not by sight.
2 Corinthians 5:7 NKJV

The Christian life has one impossibility: Hebrews 11:6 says it is impossible to please God without faith. Faith means being fully convinced that what God has promised, He will do (Romans 4:21). When adversity pressures us, doubts arise. We want to see the stairway before we lift our feet. However, God wants us to focus on what He says in His Word, not on what we feel or circumstances we see. When we believe truth, the Spirit produces the faith we need to trust God completely.

My brother, Matthew Scott Noel, learned this when diagnosed with a blocked bile duct. He wrote, "We are all on the road down the great adventure of life. The Lord has provided the directions and instructions for our purpose and plan—the Bible—but we must look up to see it. We, however, are so busy looking down at each footstep, each little pebble and pothole, we aren't even enjoying the trip! We need to look up to our eternal destiny and get our eyes focused on Jesus. Only then can we totally walk by faith and not by sight."

When Matthew died at age thirty-six, his wife Gina said, "The only way we can learn trust and obedience is to have things happen that we cannot understand. Faith begins in the dark."

To be faithful in everything, we must walk life's road by what we know of God in His Word, not by evidence we can see—that's how we please God.

Reaping after Forty Years

Faithful is He who calls you,
and He also will bring it to pass.
1 Thessalonians 5:24 NASB

I have no recollection of accepting Christ as my Savior—however, from age five, I knew I would go to heaven when I died!

When my mother was dying in 1992, we went through old photos together. One large black-and-white picture had the caption "Daily Vacation Bible School 1952." In it I am sitting on the steps outside a church with all the other students and teachers. I realized the picture was taken when I was five years old. A teacher who was clasping a Bible looked familiar. Mother told me her name was Helen Bowser, so I phoned her and asked, "Do you remember leading a five-year-old girl to Christ at DVBS forty years ago?"

"No," she answered, "but I always taught the five-year-olds."

I told her, "I think you explained salvation to me at DVBS, and I responded, but the details did not stick in my memory."

Helen was overjoyed. At the end of our conversation she said, "I'm seventy-five years old. I wasn't going to help with DVBS this year, but now I've changed my mind."

Helen Bowser was faithful over the years in working at her church. She will not know all the fruit of her labor until she enters glory, but she found out about one harvest forty years later.

No wonder I have a big smile on my face in that picture of me on the church steps.

Finishing Well

*"His master replied, 'Well done, good and faithful
servant! You have been faithful with a few
things; I will put you in charge of many things.
Come and share your master's happiness!'"*
MATTHEW 25:21 NIV

What does faithfulness look like? Showing up for
church every Sunday? Tithing on our incomes?
Preparing packages for orphans every Christmas?
These are commendable, but is that what Jesus
meant when He described "good and faithful"
servants? In one parable Jesus tells in Matthew
25, two servants doubled the talents their master
had given them, while another servant buried
his talents. Jesus called him "wicked and lazy."
The servants who were faithful to use what the
master had given them were rewarded with more
responsibilities. When talking about faithful and
wise managers, Jesus said, "From everyone who
has been given much, much will be demanded"
(Luke 12:48 NIV).

Faithfulness means using what God gives us in ways that please Him. When we serve God with our opportunities, talents and abilities, time, money, and even our spiritual insights and knowledge of God's Word, He gives us more to use for Him. But we have to guard against becoming lazy and failing to use the resources God has given us to minister to others.

John W. Thompson and Randy Scruggs wrote a beautiful praise chorus titled "Sanctuary." One verse summarizes the result of faithfulness: "When our Lord comes with shouts of glory, and our race on earth is run. How I long to hear my Lord say: 'Faithful servant, well done!'"

Are you God's good and faithful servant?

Our Calling

God is faithful, by whom you were called into
the fellowship of his Son, Jesus Christ our Lord.
1 CORINTHIANS 1:9 ESV

We often think of our calling as a ministry or location—someone is "called" to Indonesia or to work with youth. However, our main calling is not to tasks but to a mind-set. We are called to fellowship with Christ. This takes no training or education, costs no money or extra time, and has no age limits. Yes, it takes discipline, but it simply means talking with Jesus throughout the day.

A self-driven person, Sandra wanted to glorify God with her life. She prayed that she could do something great for Him and enjoyed coordinating the women's ministries at her church. Until her husband got laid off. She took a part-time job, giving up her main church responsibility, but she still wrote a Christian blog several times a week. Then her aging mother stopped driving, and

Sandra became her chauffeur. The blog got put on hold.

Sandra was frustrated until she realized that the "work" God wanted her to do for Him was different from the work she wanted to do for God. In fact, it was work she didn't even want at first. But God was working *in* her more than *through* her. Her calling was to fellowship with Jesus while she helped her husband, cared for her mother, and carried out her daily responsibilities.

Like Sandra, we can be faithful to the work God has given us. Circumstances will change as the seasons of our life progress, but we must pursue our calling to fellowship with Christ every day.

Meekness Is Good

O hope of every contrite heart,
O joy of all the meek,
To those who ask, how kind
Thou art, how good to those who seek!

TRANSLATED BY EDWARD CASWALL,
"JESUS, THE VERY THOUGHT OF THEE"

Our Meek and Lowly Example

*"Take My yoke upon you and learn
from Me, for I am gentle and lowly in
heart, and you will find rest for your souls."*
MATTHEW 11:29 NKJV

When Jesus invited His followers to take His yoke and learn from His example, He described Himself as gentle and lowly in heart. The word *gentle* in Matthew 11:29 comes from the same Greek word as *meekness* in Galatians 5:23. Of all His qualities, why did Jesus showcase meekness and humility? Consider two possible reasons:

1. It contrasted with the heavy burden of keeping the law that the religious leaders were placing on the Jews of that day (Matthew 23:4–5).
2. Jesus is not an overbearing Master. As our yoke-partner He leads us like a loving shepherd not a cattle driver. Being meek did not make him weak, however. He

bravely denounced religious hypocrisy and false teachings, and forcefully dealt with greed in the temple. But His motive was not public praise. He glorified His Father not Himself.

We learn from Him how to be meek and lowly instead of self-promoting and arrogant with our coworkers, relatives, neighbors, and church friends as He enables us. When we take Jesus' invitation and submit to His yoke, we get rest—the absence of weariness and anxiety—for our souls. Partnering with Christ to work in His kingdom gives us soul-rest. If relief for your soul sounds good to you, then consciously put on Christ's yoke of fellowship every day when you get dressed and shoulder your responsibilities.

Our Shepherd as a Sheep

He was oppressed, and he was afflicted, yet he
opened not his mouth; like a lamb that is led to
the slaughter, and like a sheep that before its
shearers is silent, so he opened not his mouth.
ISAIAH 53:7 ESV

The prophecy in Isaiah that Jesus would be
silent before his executioners not only portrays
His meekness, but also His love, patience, and
self-control. Because He loves us, He endured
oppression and affliction patiently. By His
self-control He did not defend Himself. And
He meekly allowed His torturers to lead Him
to slaughter, saying nothing. Meekness means
submitting without a struggle. He accepted His
Father's will like a sheep being sheared, even
though He could have called for angels to deliver
Him (Matthew 26:53).

Many times in life we face similar choices.
When death steals our dream or our loved one,

the Holy Spirit can give us the meekness to say, "God's will be done." When oppression and affliction plague us, we can submit because God gives us the grace to exchange our weakness for His strength. When we don't understand why we must endure trials, we can still surrender like Jesus did and learn the discipline of obedience through suffering.

Unlike Jesus, we often suffer because of our wrong choices or sinful actions. We must realize how these things grieve God. To restore fellowship, we have to confess our sins to Him and ask forgiveness from those we have wronged. God will provide the meekness we need to please our Shepherd. Are you feeling betrayed? Falsely accused? Mocked? Put down? Misunderstood? You are in good company—let Jesus' example teach you to endure. Meekly offer your suffering up to God.

Giving Not Grabbing

*"Behold, your King is coming to you, lowly,
and sitting on a donkey, a colt, the foal of a donkey."*
MATTHEW 21:5 NKJV

On a practical level, what does it take to be lowly
(meek)? What would be our cultural parallel to
riding on a small donkey? It means not promoting
ourselves at another's expense, not grabbing the
best place in line, not looking out for number one.
It means seeking ways to serve others rather than
waiting for others to serve us.

I imagine that when Jesus walked into a room,
His approach was not "Here I am you lucky
people." His attitude was "There you are, my
valued friends."

As the Holy Spirit grows the fruit of
Christlikeness in us, we will learn to focus on what
others need instead of our own self-interests.
We will ride in the middle of the backseat, leave
the best piece of chicken for someone else, clean

a house-bound friend's bathroom, work in the toddler nursery, pick up litter on a hiking trail, volunteer. DWJWD (Do What Jesus Would Do!).

Jesus rode the donkey's colt in order to fulfill the prophecy of Zechariah 9:9. On the heels of that triumphant entry where people praised Him, He took off His robe and donned a servant's towel to wash dirty feet. He had told His disciples that His purpose in life was to minister, not to be ministered to (Mark 10:45). Our Lord and teacher purposely humbled Himself to do even the lowliest job. The Holy Spirit empowers us to do the same.

Our Beauty Secret

*Your beauty should not come from outward
adornment. . . . Rather, it should be that of your inner
self, the unfading beauty of a gentle [meek] and quiet
spirit, which is of great worth in God's sight.*
1 PETER 3:3–4 NIV

A failed medical procedure permanently
paralyzed one side of RyLee's face at age twenty-
three. After a struggle, she submitted to God and
said, "My physical beauty is damaged, so I need to
concentrate on inner beauty." By God's grace she
has a meek and quiet spirit. Even though another
procedure went terribly wrong five months later
and gave her a massive stroke in the language area
of her brain.

Seven years after that, RyLee has retrained
herself to read, understand most conversations,
and write (left-handed since her right hand was
affected). When she gets discouraged by her
disabilities, she focuses on what she can do, and

in a few hours she's thankful again. RyLee's inner beauty shows up in the way she has accepted God's new assignment for her. Before the stroke she typed 120 words per minute, wrote poetry, drew fashion designs, and loved to pray. Now her vocabulary is about 250 words, but the Holy Spirit is her inner fashion designer, making her the most content gal I know. Her attitude exemplifies the meekness that should adorn all Christian women. RyLee doesn't long for what she used to have or dream about what she could have had. She accepts what she does have as God's gift and the way He will glorify Himself.[19]

Eventually, we all will lose what the world prizes as physical beauty. As we cultivate acceptance (meekness), we will keep becoming more beautiful in God's eyes.

Bless You

"Blessed are the meek, for they will inherit the earth."
MATTHEW 5:5 NIV

The purpose of fruit is not to look nice or to
benefit the plant. The purpose is to nourish
those who eat it. Yet Jesus did assign benefits
for meekness, for righteousness (goodness), and
for peacemaking (Matthew 5:3–12). First, He
said with these qualities we are blessed—happy,
fortunate.

Another benefit to meekness—a proper view
of ourselves—is that God says the meek will
inherit the earth. Inheriting land is an important
Old Testament theme. God's promise to Abraham
in Genesis 12:1–3 included what we call the
Promised Land. His descendents eventually did
live there. Unfortunately they turned away to false
gods, so God gave them the consequence of a *time
out* of the land.

Thus when Jesus said the meek would inherit the earth, it reminded them of God's covenant with their ancestor Abraham. Perhaps they also recalled Psalm 37, which says that the wicked will be cut off, but the meek will inherit the land and enjoy great peace (v. 11; also verses 18, 22, 29, 34). Not only does God produce meekness in us when we depend on Him, He rewards and blesses us for it!

Study Psalm 37 by listing the commands in verses 1–8. Then make a grid with three columns titled "What the righteous do," "What the wicked do," and "Results of those practices." This will give you insight into what delights God (v. 23) when we delight in Him (v. 4).

Meekness in Action

Brothers and sisters, if someone is caught in a sin, you who
live by the Spirit should restore that person gently.
But watch yourselves, or you also may be tempted.
GALATIANS 6:1 NIV

This verse tells us how to help someone who has
been overtaken by sin. First, we must be walking
by the Spirit when we deal with sin in others. The
word *restore* implies skill or know-how—it is also
used to describe mending fishing nets or setting
broken bones. We must be spiritually grounded
ourselves before we confront others.

Second, we need a gentle, or meek, spirit.
How do we fend off superiority when dealing
with someone who needs help? By considering
ourselves as sinners, too. We are not immune from
yielding to the same temptations and failures that
others have experienced, and we can lift them up
only through God's grace. The importance of
this spirit of meekness is stressed in Galatians

6:3, "For if anyone thinks he is something when he is nothing, he deceives himself" (NASB). We are all indebted to God's grace for all our accomplishments.

Third, we must "bear one another's burdens" (v. 2 NASB). This means being an accountability partner. Our continued involvement will help the person recover lost ground and resist future temptations.

Meekness has no conceit in it. Instead of patting ourselves on the back, we exult over what God has done in and through us. If we can help someone else, it is because God gives us the ability and insight, as well as the meekness necessary to do it.

Polished Gemstones

"But He knows the way that I take;
when He has tested me, I shall come forth as gold."
JOB 23:10 NKJV

Stones polished in a tumbler become smooth
and shiny from the friction of rubbing against
each other. To polish us, God sometimes gives
more than we can bear. While 1 Corinthians 10:13
promises we will not be tempted beyond our
endurance because we can escape by saying no, in
2 Corinthians 1:8–9, Paul and Timothy said, "We
were burdened beyond measure, above strength,
so that we despaired even of life. . . . [In order]
that we should not trust in ourselves but in God
who raises the dead" (NKJV).

When everything is good, we think we do
not need God. Without stress, we are peaceful on
our own. However, we learn peace and patience
from tribulation. Likewise, it is easy to be kind
to those who treat us kindly. God might put
unlovely people in our lives so we learn to love

like Jesus. Because of sorrow we appreciate joy. By experiencing temptation, we gain self-control. And by giving us more than we think we can bear, He makes us meek. Meekness means accepting God's "dealings with us as good, and therefore without disputing or resisting."[20]

God is our wise and loving coach. He disciplines us with rigorous training to develop our spiritual muscles. Like a doctor who must hurt in order to heal, He knows what we need to keep us from trusting in ourselves. As polished stones, we can shine for His glory.

Benefits of Failure

Now the man Moses was very meek, more than
all people who were on the face of the earth.
NUMBERS 12:3 ESV

$\mathscr{P}$erhaps Moses' meekness stemmed from his
attempt early in life to avenge the mistreatment of
his people by murdering an Egyptian taskmaster.
That sent him into hiding for forty years, and
instead of ruling Egypt, he ruled a flock of sheep
in the wilderness. But God didn't waste those
years of exile. Moses learned wilderness survival
skills, which he would need later while wandering
the desert for forty years with the Israelites. That
early failure must have taught him that he could
not do God's work in his own way, by his own
efforts. When God eventually recruited him at
the burning bush, Moses reluctantly accepted
his part in God's rescue plan for Israel. He also
demonstrated meekness when he took his father-
in-law's advice (Exodus 18) and when he offered

God his life for the rebellious and murmuring people he was leading (Exodus 32:30–32; Numbers 14:11–21).

Maybe you have defined yourself by a significant failure in your past. But rather than sabotaging your ability to serve God, it can be a catalyst to make you a meek servant that God can use. Moses had a proper view of his need for dependence on God, was open to advice, and was willing to sacrifice himself for others. Because of this he communed with God face-to-face like a friend. Let your significant failures teach you the meekness you need to allow God to do His work His way, and to help you enjoy personal communion with Him.

Weeping Produces Meekness

The LORD *is near to the brokenhearted*
and saves those who are crushed in spirit.
PSALM 34:18 NASB

Having a "good cry" is not an oxymoron; crying is therapeutic. Of all living creatures, only humans cry. Crying is a God-given outlet for emotion, and it helps us realize our need for Him. How many different biblical people shed tears? At least forty, including Jesus. However, tears embarrass us. They make our faces puffy and our noses red—and what if we don't have a tissue? Tears make us feel inferior, inadequate, and powerless.

Though unwelcome intruders, tears serve valuable purposes. Physically, they relieve tension and express grief and pain. Spiritually, they compel us to give up our self-sufficiency for God-dependency. Elisabeth Elliot said, "The will is surrendered through the tear ducts." Tears can produce meekness and help us accept difficulties and give our brokenness to God. Like a child taking her shattered toy to her dad to fix, we must surrender all our broken pieces to our Father God. Tears make us willing to do that. They empty us of self-will so God can fill the void with what He wills. He promises to draw near to us when we draw near to Him (James 4:8). God values our tears. "You have. . .put my tears in Your bottle. Are they not in Your book?" (Psalm 56:8 NASB).

As a rainstorm refreshes and nourishes nature, so weeping is good for us physically, emotionally, and spiritually. Let yourself have a "good cry" whenever and wherever it happens.

Self-Control Takes
PATIENCE

We go wrong because we stubbornly refuse to discipline ourselves physically, morally, or mentally.

OSWALD CHAMBERS, *My Utmost for His Highest*

Self-Talk Control

Casting down arguments and every high thing that exalts itself against the knowledge of God, bringing every thought into captivity to the obedience of Christ. . .
2 CORINTHIANS 10:5 NKJV

$\mathcal{B}$ecause our hearts are desperately wicked and will deceive us, some of our self-talk will be wicked and deceptive also. *I know I shouldn't have another piece of fried chicken, but it is so yummy, and I can't resist.* This kind of self-talk is based on feelings and should be challenged: *I'm not stuffed, but I'm no longer hungry—I'm satisfied, so I'll push my plate away and stop eating now, before I regret the extra calories.*

Here's another example of deceptive self-talk: *People at church don't talk to me. All the pastor does is shake my hand and move me on. It's a good church and I like the teaching, but maybe it's not the right fit for me.* By exercising self-control over our thinking, we can catch these negative attitudes and change them in obedience to Christ: *O Lord, I know I shouldn't be critical and blame the church for my problems. Help me to be friendly and make the first move. Show me how I can get involved and serve at this church, not just expect others to serve me.*

We have to train ourselves to recognize negative and dangerous self-talk and refuse to listen to it. What areas of your thinking need this kind of self-control? The Holy Spirit will help us talk ourselves into obeying instead of listening to our thoughts when they argue against God's principles.

Making Every Effort

*For this very reason, make every effort to add to
your faith goodness; and to goodness, knowledge;
and to knowledge, self-control; and to self-control,
perseverance; and to perseverance, godliness; and to
godliness, mutual affection; and to mutual affection,
love. For if you possess these qualities in increasing
measure, they will keep you from being ineffective and
unproductive in your knowledge of our Lord Jesus Christ.*
2 Peter 1:5–8 niv

Self-control does not come naturally. We are
like the little girl who sat down when her mother
insisted but said, "I'm still standing up on the
inside."

Ideally, as preschoolers we learn self-control
by submitting to our parents. Then, as we develop
a relationship with our heavenly Father, we learn
to surrender to His control. We can see this
progression in Peter's writings. Peter was probably
the apostle who had the least self-control at first.

He often spoke impulsively, and Jesus at one time called his idea satanic (Matthew 16:23).

However, Peter learned that "His divine power has granted to us everything pertaining to life and godliness, through the true knowledge of Him who called us by His own glory and excellence" (2 Peter 1:3 NASB). Because we share God's nature, we have His divine power to resist evil and live a godly life. When we "make every effort" to add self-control to our faith, goodness, and knowledge, we will be useful and fruitful in knowing and living for Christ. Second Peter tells us to make every effort to control ourselves and increase in spiritual virtues, and we can do this by relying on God's power and grace (2 Corinthians 3:5). Becoming a self-controlled Christian requires submitting to God's control instead of trying to run our lives without Him. Don't be like a rebellious child—bow to God on the inside as well as the outside.

Staying Inbounds

Everyone who competes in the games goes into strict training.
They do it to get a crown that will not last, but we do it to get
a crown that will last forever. . . . No, I strike a blow to my
body and make it my slave so that after I have preached to
others, I myself will not be disqualified for the prize.
1 CORINTHIANS 9:25, 27 NIV

We usually think of Paul as being fully devoted to God, so how could he be concerned about disqualification? He took the Gospel to the then-known world, received God's revelation to write at least thirteen books of the New Testament, and told Christians to follow his example. Consequently he gained notoriety and fame. He must have realized how easily people with power can take advantage of their positions. They begin to think rules don't apply to them, that they can take liberties.

Paul might have been susceptible to letting pride go to his head, because God gave him a thorn in the flesh to torment him, so he would not exalt himself. When God answered no to his fervent prayers for healing, he became glad for this affliction, because it kept him dependent on God's power and strength. It taught him the sufficiency of God's grace (2 Corinthians 12:7–10).

Paul wrote, "If anyone competes as an athlete, he does not win the prize unless he competes according to the rules" (2 Timothy 2:5 NASB). Like Paul, we need self-control in everything, so we will not step over the lines or break any rules. We all know Christians who have fallen, and we are not immune to temptation either. Strive to exercise self-control over your passions, thoughts, appetites, and pursuits, and remember that the Holy Spirit will help you.

What Should I Wear?

*That you put off, concerning your former conduct,
the old man which grows corrupt according to the deceitful
lusts, and be renewed in the spirit of your mind, and that
you put on the new man which was created according to
God, in true righteousness and holiness. . .*

EPHESIANS 4:22–24 NKJV

❧

"Clothes make the man!" Mark Twain said. He
meant that what we wear affects how we feel
about ourselves and how we act. A recent wedding
invitation included this notation: *semiformal attire
requested.* Because the wedding was a formal
occasion held in an elegantly decorated church,
the bride and groom wanted their guests'
experience to match the setting.

The New Testament tells us to "put off"
the works of the flesh and sinful deeds and
conformity to the world, and instead "put on"
the works of the Spirit, resulting in holiness.
This takes self-control, which starts with mind
control. "Be renewed in the spirit of your mind"

(Ephesians 4:23 NKJV). Right thinking helps us dress appropriately with right conduct. First Peter 1:13 says, "Gird up the loins of your mind" (NKJV). This verse illustrates tucking up one's robes in order to run or take action. When we gather up and control our thoughts, self-controlled behavior results. If we have undisciplined habits, we should examine our thought-life. What we think and believe determines what we do, in the same way that what we wear affects how we behave.

If you need to break a habit, ask God to reveal where your thinking is wrong. Then saturate your mind with God's truth about the behavior you desire. When wrong thoughts enter, replace them with God's Word. As we put off our former desires, we will put on holy conduct—that's what the best-dressed Christian woman wears.

Are You Being Sanctified?

*As obedient children, do not be conformed to the
passions of your former ignorance, but as he who
called you is holy, you also be holy in all your conduct.*
1 PETER 1:14–15 ESV

Children must be trained to obey. Rewarding
good behavior programs their brains to repeat
what was rewarded. And when mothers
express disapproval or other consequences
for misbehavior, their children learn to stop
disobeying.

God trains His children, too, in a process
called *sanctification*—being made holy or set
apart. God wants us separated from sinfulness
and impurity. "For this is the will of God, your
sanctification: that you abstain from sexual
immorality. . . . For God has not called us for
impurity, but in holiness" (1 Thessalonians 4:3,
7 ESV). God's will for your life includes sexual
purity. How do we abstain from immorality in
thought and conduct? By self-control. Every day

we are tempted to stray, to disobey, to flirt with sin—and sin is attractive. It does provide pleasure. Sometimes we ignore the consequences and give in. Resisting temptations requires us to take our passions under control and snap our minds back to reality by calling on God to help us.

Why is this so important, besides being God's will? Because sin breaks our fellowship with God, we will always regret it, and unconfessed sin escalates and leads to new sins. Secret sin is impossible—God knows about it, and you know about it. Sin can be forgiven, but some consequences are permanent.

We must deal quickly and drastically with temptation. Fellowship with Christ enables us to control ourselves as the Spirit's fruit grows in us.

Desiring the Lord

*Delight yourself in the LORD, and he will give
you the desires of your heart. Commit your way
to the LORD; trust in him, and he will act.*
PSALM 37:4–5 ESV

"I'm not a self-disciplined person," Peg confessed
to her friend Janet. "God made my personality
more free-spirited and spontaneous. So I know I
should read the Bible every day and not stay out
past midnight on Saturday evenings, because then
I don't feel like getting up for church, but I'm not
all regimented and scheduled like some of God's
children."

"You're right," Janet said. "God loves and
accepts you the way you are, but let me ask you
something. Why do you wash your hair every
morning?"

"So it doesn't feel icky!"

"Reading your Bible would take less effort
than washing and styling your hair," Janet

continued. "How often do you clean your apartment?"

"Every Friday or Saturday."

"It takes self-discipline to do that. You probably watch certain TV programs every week. Why can't you fellowship with God's people and be encouraged from His Word a couple hours on Sundays? Besides, the church body needs your ministry, too."

"You're right," Peg said. "If I want something bad enough, I do it. I guess I have a desire problem more than a discipline problem."

"We all do. But when we delight in the Lord—make Him our priority—He will give us the desires He wants us to have."

Peg looked thoughtful. "Maybe that's why the fruit of the Spirit includes self-control. If I please God, not myself, the Holy Spirit will help me do what I should."

"Sounds like a plan," Janet said. "Let's pray about it right now."

Obedience Requires Self-Control

He replied, "My mother and brothers are those who hear God's word and put it into practice."
LUKE 8:21 NIV

Self-control is more than restraining myself from sinning or doing harm. Self-control is also disciplined behavior that obeys God's commands. Jesus had a repeated theme when He taught: don't merely hear God's word—do it. His Sermon on the Mount ended with an illustration of building a house on rock not sand. Jesus compared having this rock-solid foundation to putting His words into practice (Matthew 7:24–27). Jesus' parable about the sower described four types of soil that the seed of God's Word can fall on: hard, rocky, thorny, and good. He wanted us to recognize that every time we hear God's truth, we will have one of four responses to it. If our hearts are hard (closed), Satan will steal the seed. With rocky (calloused) or thorny (crowded) hearts, we will not follow through, and the seed will die. But when our hearts are good (cultivated), we nurture the seed so it grows and produces fruit containing more seeds of God's truth for us to disperse.

James 1:22–25 compares hearing God's Word but not doing it to looking in a mirror and immediately forgetting what we look like. Being a fruitful Christian requires more than hearing and understanding God's truth. We must also do what it says. I may have ears that hear and a head that knows, but I also need hands that act.

Being Precedes Doing

"These people draw near to Me with their mouth,
and honor Me with their lips, but their heart is
far from Me. And in vain they worship Me,
teaching as doctrines the commandments of men."
MATTHEW 15:8–9 NKJV

The choice to obey and worship is ours. While obedience is our obligation, our efforts are not without God's help. We step into the water, and then God parts it. But God wants more than adherence to rules and rituals. He wants our hearts. Do you ever take a walk to meditate on God (no earbuds allowed)? Can you sit on your porch with only your Bible in your lap and your phone turned off? Perhaps you have a meaningful worship experience in church, but God wants our worship every day. We can meditate on Him while we're working in our kitchens, stuck in traffic, or shopping at the mall. Some of our best fellowship may occur in a birthing room or while sitting in a dental chair or pre-op waiting room. Medical needs send us to God's lap.

The biblical word *worship* does not mean "praise." It means "prostration." Worship is more about surrendering than about getting a good feeling. We should focus on God seeing our hearts, not on people seeing how sincerely we sing praise songs in church. Job worshipped when he bowed to the ground and said, "The LORD gave, and the LORD has taken away; blessed be the name of the LORD" (Job 1:20–21 NKJV).

It takes self-control to worship God when we're suffering. In your present circumstances, are you bowing your knee to God or shaking your fist at Him? The Holy Spirit will help you respond with a heart of worship.

Sanctification Hurts but Helps

That you may walk worthy of the Lord,
fully pleasing Him, being fruitful in every good
work and increasing in the knowledge of God. . .
COLOSSIANS 1:10 NKJV

In the spring, grapevines must be cut back so
that only four branches grow out from the main
stalk. These branches will send out numerous
canes with large green leaves. Then little grape
clusters begin to form. In midsummer, the canes
need pruning so growth goes to the fruit instead
of the leaves. In much the same way, the fruit of
the Spirit grows best through pruning. God wants
to cut away our inflated view of self and deliver
us from a bloated sense of our own importance,
so our focus will be on God's glory. Even the
Holy Spirit does not glorify Himself—He glorifies
Christ (John 16:14). The pruning process of

sanctification achieves that result in us.

But sanctification is a two-sided coin: God's part—"It is God who works in you both to will and to do for His good pleasure" (Philippians 2:13 NKJV). Our responsibility—"That you may become blameless and harmless, children of God without fault in the midst of a crooked and perverse generation" (Philippians 2:15 NKJV). We grow in holiness through spiritual workouts, often involving difficulties. "I am being poured out as a drink offering on the sacrifice and service of your faith" (Philippians 2:17 NKJV).

The purpose of sanctification is for us to "worship God in the Spirit, rejoice in Christ Jesus, and have no confidence in the flesh" (Philippians 3:3 NKJV). Are you hurting? Remember, God's pruning produces fruit when we worship, rejoice, and give up self-reliance.

Notes

1. Steve Herzig, "Jewish Worship," accessed August 28, 2012, www.foigm.org/free-resources/article/jewish-worship/.
2. www.5lovelanguages.com
3. With special thanks to Anna Zogg for her insights.
4. Earl D. Radmacher and Ronald B. Allen, eds., *The Nelson Study Bible, New King James Version* (Nashville, TN: Thomas Nelson, 1997).
5. Joni Eareckson Tada, *Heaven, Your Real Home* (Grand Rapids, MI: Zondervon, 1995), 190–191.
6. With thanks to Leah Gingery for her insights on *shalom* and *aloha*.
7. www.AgapeLandMusic.com
8. With special thanks to Esther Hayden for her insights.
9. Marcia Hornok, originally published in *Discipleship Journal* (Nov/Dec 1990).
10. With thanks to Pauline Thacher for this illustration.
11. "What's Love Got to Do With It?" *The Sunday News*, February 13, 2011 (2011 Amy Writing Awards).
12. With gratitude to Marcia Lindelien for her insights.
13. James Reimann, ed., *My Utmost for His Highest: The Golden Book of Oswald Chambers*, May 2.
14. With gratitude to Esther Hayden for her insights.
15. The author gratefully acknowledges insights on Ruth from Dr. Amber Warhurst.
16. With thanks to Leah Gingery for her insights.
17. Insights gleaned from *CHERA Fellowship* magazine published by IFCA International.
18. "Overheard in an Orchard," author unknown.
19. Told with permission from Nathan and RyLee Hornok.
20. W. E. Vine, *Expository Dictionary of New Testament Words*, vol. 3, p. 55.